GERMAN COOKING

Ruth Malinowski

Patricia Sinclair   Alinda Nelson

WEATHERVANE
BOOKS

The authors wish to thank our German friend Anni Schneider for her valuable assistance.

The following picture was provided through the courtesy of Transworld Feature Syndicate, Inc.:
Studio Conti: p. 11

contents

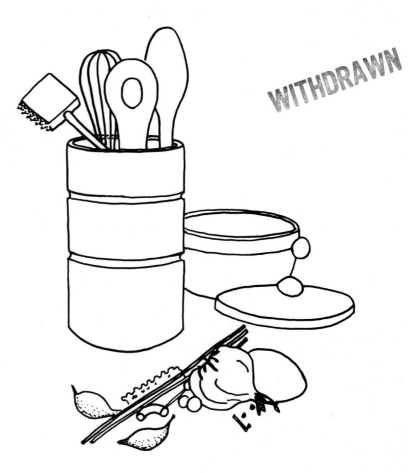

Introduction to German Cooking	4
Soups	7
Luncheon Dishes	13
Meat, Poultry, Game, and Fish	17
Vegetables	41
Salads	47
Breads, Dumplings, and Spaetzle	54
Cookies	57
Desserts and Cakes	62
Special-Occasion Dishes	75
Index	79

introduction to german cooking

German cooking is good, plain cooking — down-to-earth, simple, and substantial. Foods are prepared that go well with their popular thirst-quenchers, beer and wine.

Most nations incorporate local home-grown foods into their eating pattern. Such is also the case in Germany, where vegetables such as snow-white cauliflower, green cabbages, perfect asparagus, and red, juicy tomatoes grow in abundance. These succulent vegetables are used alone or in delicious combinations.

German dairy and meat products are of highest quality. Sides of pigs, calves, and beef yield top-grade roasts, hams, chops, and a vast array of tasty sausages. Seafood, fresh from the North Sea and the Baltic, is bountiful in the northern area of Germany. Herring, lobster, sole, and bass are typical fare. Inland streams produce river salmon and brook trout.

Bakers using local grains are famous for regional specialties such as breads of various shapes and colors, pastries, and a wide variety of Christmas sweets.

The hop fields and wine hills have given Germany some of their major exports. German beer is truly outstanding and has won praise around the world. Most towns have their own brewery and home cooks prepare foods, such as soup, roasts, and fritters, which go well with beer. Foods are often cooked in beer for a distinct and improved flavor. Although Germany is most famous for its beer, many German wines are second to none. Best known are the white wines, such as Rhine and Moselle. Many red wines are considered very good also. A less well-known cuisine of Germany is associated with these fine red and white wines. These foods include Rhine Salmon or Cucumber salad — elegant and sophisticated.

cuisines of france versus germany

The cuisines of France and Germany are very different and reflect the major drinking habits of each country. Because most Germans are beer-drinkers rather than wine-drinkers, their foods are more substantial and generally without frills. For example, the French will spend hours making a light puff pastry, whereas the Germans prepare heavier desserts that could be an entire light meal for an American. German people come to the dinner table expecting hearty foods.

german influence on american fare

German foods have had a tremendous influence on American cooking. The United States national favorite, the frankfurter, can be traced to the German sausage. Hamburger, a second United States favorite, was developed in Hamburg, Germany. In this book you will recognize other foods that sound very American but which originated in Germany. Because German foods tend to be generally bland, they are very suitable to the American taste. Some of the other European countries have highly spiced foods which Americans enjoy occasionally but not as everyday fare.

description of courses
appetizers

German lunches or dinners consist of several courses. Although hors d'oeuvres are not as popular as in some countries, they are often served. Soft cheese encircled by chopped onions may be served with slices of pumpernickel bread. Salads, particularly herring, large enough to be an entree may also be served.

soups

Most families omit the hors d'oeuvres and start their luncheons or dinners with a soup. Very popular are thick soups such as potato, cabbage, or bean. Sausage and onion may give these soups a distinct flavor. Clear soups with large or small dumplings are popular, as are creamy soups such as asparagus or seafood bisque. One national favorite is eel soup. Spaetzle, a type of noodle, is often served in soup in place of dumplings. A spaetzle machine cuts the dough in many sizes and shapes. In lieu of a machine, the dough can be forced through the holes of a colander into boiling water.

meats

Meat dishes are a staple of German meals. Of these, the pot roast method of cooking is most popular. Pork, fresh or cured, is the number one favorite, and German cooks prepare it in dozens of ways. Veal is next in popularity and is cooked as roasts or as cutlets called schnitzel. Meats are often marinated and then pot-roasted. Sweet-and-sour sauce is prepared by a vinegar-based marinade, with sugar added during cooking. The frequent use of fruit, especially dried fruit, makes meat-cooking different from other countries. Often a fruit compote from dried apples, pears, prunes, and apricots may accompany meat. Only small amounts of herbs are used to flavor meat dishes. Among the most popular are parsley, bay leaf and marjoram. Fresh dill is used more often with fish than meat. Caraway seeds and curry also are used.

Variety meats are esteemed in Germany. Tongue, heart, liver, and sweetbreads are enjoyed. Game is served often and is prepared by roasting or braising. Holiday meals may be planned around a pheasant, partridge, or rabbit. Goose and duck in Germany are meaty compared with fat American birds. Chickens, roasted, sautéed, or boiled, are popular.

Three hundred different kinds of sausages are the basis of German delicatessen foods. Frozen bratwurst, the pork sausage of Nuremberg, to the hearty Berliner sausage, each region has its own specialty. Each is distinctly different and marvelously tasty. Other delicatessen specialties are ready-to-serve salads and a variety of potato dishes.

fish

Fish dishes may be plain or fancy. A sour-cream sauce or a rich sweet-and-sour sauce with raisins accompany some fish. Of course, herring is extremely popular and is served in every imaginable form — fried, pickled, or in salads, for instance. Bluefish is interesting in that the "blue" refers to the cooking method, not to the fish. Trout, salmon, carp, or other fish are marinated and cooked in a vinegar solution. This turns the skin to a blue color and blanches the flesh white. A tart fish sauce usually accompanies this dish.

main-dish accompaniments

Certain vegetables, such as cucumbers, asparagus, cabbage, and mushrooms, are prepared in many ways and are served frequently. Most typically German is sauerkraut. This specialty may be served in some families two or three times a day, hot or cold, and varied by the addition of wine, caraway seeds, or apples. Regional differences and personal preferences determine the recipe. Sauerkraut is rinsed with warm water and drained well.

Dumplings and potatoes are a part of almost every meal. Sauces or gravies are served on meats, and fruit-preserve relishes are present at most meals.

breads and sweets

Bread is very much a basic staple. Northern Germany uses its local grains, rye and barley, to produce solid dark breads. Central and southern Germany produce more fancy baking from their locally grown wheat.

Because of overcrowded living conditions and a fuel shortage, little bread was baked at home in times past. This trend still continues, and local bakeries do much of the bread-baking. Sweetened breads are more often made at home. Honey cakes and fruit breads derive their sweetness from the honey and dried fruits rather than from white sugar.

Special Christmas baking is a long-standing tradition. Several weeks before Christmas commercial bakers and homemakers start cooking for the holidays. Many of these traditional recipes are included in the book.

desserts and pastries

Germans usually serve fresh fruit, a fruit compote, a custard, or a pudding for dessert. Apples are the fruit used most frequently. A large mound of whipped cream garnishes these desserts. Pastries are popular, but not for dessert. Late-afternoon coffee or tea is accompanied by a baked treat.

five meals a day

Germans eat five times each day. Breakfast is fairly hearty — a boiled egg, rolls, dark bread, a little meat or cheese, and a large amount of fresh coffee. In midmorning a second breakfast is served, and it may be a meat sandwich, sausage, and a salad.

The noon dinner is traditionally the largest meal of the day and consists of the following: soup with noodles or dumplings, a roast, potatoes, vegetables, sauerkraut, and a fruit dessert. Now this meal often is served in the evening if the housewife is working. A light cafeteria meal may be purchased at noon by working family members.

Late afternoon means coffee time. Little sandwiches, cakes, or tarts are served at home or enjoyed in the local pastry shops.

A simple evening meal of bread, cheese, and cold cuts is served later if the large meal was eaten at noon. Beer accompanies most of the larger meals.

regional cooking

Each region of Germany has its own culinary specialties. Many of the more-popular recipes are included in this book. A few of the regional specialties are listed here.

Berlin — strongly flavored soups, such as pea soup with bacon, cauliflower dishes, jelly doughnuts (invented in Berlin), and schnapps.

Northern and Eastern area of West Germany — delicious fresh fish, hearty soups. Hamburg is noted for poultry and ducks. Meat quality is tops.

Westphalia (near Holland) — savory casseroles using pork; world-famous for Westphalian hams (pickled and smoked).

Bavaria — beer country, and foods are designed to go well with the beer. Weisswürste sausage, strudels, and yeast dumplings are popular.

Swabia (close to Switzerland and France) — wines in this area are popular. Spaetzle (noodles) are served often.

Rhineland — white wine country. More elaborate dishes prepared to go well with wine; also famous for cookies.

special ingredients

Few special ingredients are needed for the recipes in this book. Questions might be raised about the following items.

Ground almonds — purchase at most supermarkets in the nuts section, or grind whole blanched almonds in a blender.

Vanilla butter and nut flavoring — found with the vanilla in supermarkets.

Fillo leaves (for strudel) — found frozen at many supermarkets or specialty stores.

Dark beer — ask for this at liquor stores.

Other suggestions for ingredients or special equipment are included in the recipes.

summary

Germans love to eat and drink heartily. The recipes in this book reflect this love. These foods are easy to prepare and robust in flavor without the addition of many spices. The foods are filling and generally not expensive. Use fresh, quality ingredients for best results. As you prepare and eat these foods, thousands of Germans are doing the same in their homes. Guten appetit!

soups

two-bean soup
zwei-bohnensuppe

1¼ cups dry white beans
¼ pound ham, cubed
1 cup cut green beans, fresh
    or frozen
¼ cup diced celery
1 green onion, diced
1 yellow onion, diced
1 potato, peeled and diced
1 tablespoon butter
2 tablespoons flour
¾ cup beef broth
½ teaspoon salt
¼ teaspoon pepper
1 sprig parsley for garnish

Cover white beans with cold water and soak overnight.

Drain and place beans in a 2-quart saucepan. Add ham and enough cold water to cover beans by 1 inch. Bring water to a boil and simmer for about 1 hour or until beans are tender. Add green beans, celery, onion, and potato. Add enough water to cover the vegetables; simmer for 20 minutes.

In a frypan melt butter and stir in flour. Cook, stirring until lightly browned. Remove from heat and stir in heated beef broth. Cook mixture until smooth. Stir mixture into the soup and simmer until soup is thickened and vegetables are tender. Season with salt and pepper.

Garnish with chopped parsley and serve immediately. Makes 4 to 6 servings.

white bean soup
weisse bohnensuppe

1 pound dried navy beans
3 quarts water
Smoked ham bone or ham
    hock
2 tablespoons chopped parsley
1 cup finely chopped onions
1 clove garlic, minced
2 cups finely chopped celery
    with green tops
1½ teaspoons salt
½ teaspoon pepper

Cover beans with water in large pot or soup kettle and soak overnight.

Rinse beans well and return to pot with ham bone and 3 quarts water. Simmer uncovered for 2 hours.

Add parsley, onions, garlic, celery, salt, and pepper. Simmer uncovered for 1 hour or until vegetables are tender.

Remove ham bone, dice the meat, and add meat to soup. Serve hot. Makes 8 servings.

bean soup with frankfurters
frankfurter bohnensuppe

1 pound dried navy beans
8 cups water
3 cups beef broth
1 carrot, chopped
1 celery stalk, chopped
4 strips bacon, cubed
2 small onions, chopped
1 teaspoon salt
¼ teaspoon white pepper
6 frankfurters, sliced
2 tablespoons chopped parsley

Soak beans in water overnight.

In a 3-quart saucepan bring beans, water, and beef broth to a boil. Cook for about 1 hour. Add carrot and celery and continue cooking for 30 minutes.

In a separate frypan cook the bacon until transparent. Add the onions; cook until golden. Set aside.

Mash soup through a sieve or food mill. Return to pan and add the bacon-onion mixture, salt and pepper. Add frankfurters; reheat about 5 minutes.

Sprinkle soup with chopped parsley and serve. Makes 4 to 6 servings.

cabbage soup
krautsuppe

4 thick slices bacon, diced
2 onions, sliced
1 turnip, sliced
2 carrots, diced
2 potatoes, cubed
1 small head green cabbage,
    shredded
4 cups chicken stock or bouillon
2 cups water
6 parsley sprigs and bay leaf
    tied together with thread
Salt and pepper to taste
¼ cup grated Parmesan
    cheese for garnish

In a 6-quart saucepan or pot, combine all ingredients except salt, pepper, and cheese. Simmer partially covered for 1½ to 2 hours. Discard the parsley bundle; season to taste.

Pour into hot soup plates and garnish with cheese. Makes 6 servings.

goulash soup
gulaschsuppe

2 cups chopped onion
¼ cup shortening
3 green peppers, chopped
3 tablespoons tomato paste
1 pound lean beef, cut in
   1-inch cubes
Dash red pepper

1 teaspoon paprika
2 cloves garlic, minced
½ teaspoon salt
6 cups beef broth, canned or
   homemade
1 tablespoon lemon juice
¼ teaspoon caraway seeds

Fry onions in hot fat until transparent. Add green peppers and tomato paste. Cover and simmer 10 minutes. Add meat and remaining ingredients. Simmer about 1½ hours, until meat is tender. (Add cubed potatoes if you like and simmer until potatoes are done.)

(Best when served the second day.) Makes 6 servings.

kale and potato soup
grünkohlsuppe

4 medium potatoes
2 tablespoons vegetable oil
8 cups water
1 teaspoon salt
½ teaspoon pepper
2 pounds fresh kale
½ pound cooked, sliced
   smoked garlic sausage

Peel and chop potatoes. Combine with vegetable oil and water. Cook for 20 to 30 minutes or until potatoes are tender. Remove potatoes and reserve liquid. Mash potatoes through a sieve and return to potato liquid. Add salt and pepper and simmer for 20 minutes.

Wash kale discarding all tough leaves, and cut into thin shreds. Add to potatoes and cook for 25 minutes.

Add sausage. Simmer gently for 5 minutes. Serve. Makes 6 to 8 servings.

lentil soup x
linsensuppe

1 pound dried lentils
6 slices bacon, diced
1 cup chopped onion
½ cup chopped carrots
6 cups water
1½ teaspoons salt
½ teaspoon pepper

½ teaspoon thyme
2 bay leaves
½ cup grated potato
1 ham bone or 2 smoked pork
   hocks
2 tablespoons fresh lemon
   juice

Wash and sort lentils. Soak lentils overnight or bring to a boil and boil 2 minutes. Cover and let stand 1 hour. Drain lentils.

In 4- or 5-quart Dutch oven sauté bacon until crisp. Remove bacon.

Sauté onions and carrots in bacon grease until onions are golden. Add lentils, 6 cups water, seasonings, potato, and ham bone or pork hocks. Simmer, covered, for 3 hours.

Or, in a crock pot, cook on low for 6 hours.

To serve, remove bay leaves and ham bone. Skim fat. Remove any meat from ham bone or hocks. Mash lentils slightly to thicken soup. Just before serving, stir in lemon juice. Makes 3 quarts.

lentil soup
with frankfurters
linsensuppe mit frankfurter

1 cup dried quick-cooking
   lentils
6 cups water
2 slices lean bacon, diced
1 leek or green onion, finely
   chopped
1 large carrot, finely chopped
1 celery stalk, chopped

1 onion, finely chopped
1 tablespoon vegetable oil
2 tablespoons flour
1 tablespoon vinegar
4 frankfurters, thickly sliced
1 tablespoon tomato catsup
1 teaspoon salt
¼ teaspoon black pepper

Wash the lentils thoroughly.

In a 2½-quart saucepan bring 6 cups water to a boil. Add the lentils, bacon, leek or green onion, carrot and celery. Simmer, partially covered, for 30 to 40 minutes.

Meanwhile in a frypan, sauté chopped onion in vegetable oil until soft. Sprinkle flour over onion, and stir. Lower heat, stir constantly, and cook until the flour turns light brown. Do not burn flour. Stir ½ cup of hot lentil soup into the browned flour; heat with a wire whisk until well-blended. Beat in vinegar.

Add contents of frypan to lentil pan and stir together. Cover and simmer for 30 minutes or until lentils are soft. Add the frankfurters and catsup. Cook to heat frankfurters through. Season with salt and pepper and serve hot. Makes 4 servings.

oxtail
soup
ochsenschwanzsuppe

1 2-pound disjointed oxtail or
   2 veal tails
1 medium onion, sliced
2 tablespoons vegetable oil
8 cups water
1 teaspoon salt
4 peppercorns
¼ cup chopped parsley
½ cup diced carrots
1 cup diced celery
1 bay leaf
½ cup tomatoes, drained
1 teaspoon dried thyme
1 tablespoon flour
1 tablespoon butter or
   margarine
¼ cup Madeira

In a 4-quart Dutch oven brown oxtail and onion in hot oil for several minutes. Add water, salt, and peppercorns; simmer uncovered for about 2 hours. Cover and continue to simmer for 3 additional hours. Add the parsley, carrots, celery, bay leaf, tomatoes, and thyme; continue simmering, covered, for 30 minutes longer or until the vegetables are tender.

Strain stock and refrigerate for an hour or more. In a blender puree the edible meat and vegetables and reserve. Remove fat from top of stock and reheat.

In a large, dry frypan brown flour over high heat. Cool slightly. Add the butter or margarine; blend. A little at a time, add the stock and vegetables.

Correct the seasoning and add Madeira just before serving. Makes 6 servings.

fresh tomato soup
frische tomatensuppe

6 medium-size tomatoes or
   about 2 pounds Italian
   plum tomatoes
1 onion, chopped
1 stalk celery, chopped
2 cups chicken broth
1 tablespoon tomato paste
½ teaspoon dried basil
¼ teaspoon freshly ground
   pepper
½ teaspoon salt
½ cup yogurt

Cut tomatoes into wedges and place in 1½-quart saucepan with all
ingredients except yogurt. Simmer uncovered for 30 minutes. Strain to
remove tomato skins and seeds. Adjust seasonings.

Garnish with spoonfuls of yogurt. Makes 4 to 6 servings.

fresh tomato soup

potato soup
kartoffelsuppe

2 medium potatoes
1 medium-size onion
4 stalks celery with green
   leaves
2 tablespoons vegetable oil
Boiling water
1 small bay leaf
½ teaspoon salt
2 tablespoons butter
2 to 3 cups milk
Chopped parsley for garnish

Peel and thinly slice potatoes, onion, and celery. Sauté for 3 to 5 minutes in hot vegetable oil.

In a large pot, add enough boiling water to cover vegetables. Place bay leaf and salt in pot and boil vegetables until tender. Drain vegetables and reserve liquid.

Mash vegetables into vegetable stock; add butter. Thin soup with milk as desired; heat until warm. (Do not boil.)

Ladle into soup bowls and sprinkle with chopped parsley. Makes 4 to 6 servings.

potato and cucumber soup
gurken und kartoffelsuppe

1 medium cucumber
4 medium potatoes, peeled
   and diced
1 teaspoon salt
2 cups cold water
¼ teaspoon white pepper
1 cup heavy cream
½ cup milk
1 green onion, grated
1 teaspoon dried dillweed (or
   1 tablespoon chopped fresh
   dill)

Peel the cucumber and slice it lengthwise. Scoop out seeds with a spoon and discard. Dice cucumber.

In a heavy 2½-quart saucepan boil potatoes in salted water until the potatoes are very soft. Pour potatoes and cooking liquid into a sieve or food mill set over a large bowl. Force potatoes through. Return to saucepan. Stir in pepper, cream, milk, grated onion and the cucumber. Simmer gently about 5 minutes or until the cucumber is tender.

Add dill and season to taste. Serve hot. Makes 4 servings.

luncheon dishes

onion pie
zwiebelkuchen

This is traditionally served in restaurants and wine stubes in the autumn when new wine is opened. May be served with salad for lunch.

1 package active dry yeast
1 teaspoon sugar
1½ teaspoons salt
3 to 3¼ cups unsifted flour
1 tablespoon shortening
1 cup water, 120 to 130°F
  (very warm)

6 slices bacon, cut-up
2 medium onions, sliced
¼ teaspoon cumin
½ teaspoon salt
Pepper, as desired
1 egg yolk
1 cup sour cream

Mix yeast, sugar, 1 teaspoon salt, and ½ cup flour. Blend in shortening and warm water. Beat for 2 minutes. Add enough flour to make a soft dough. Knead dough until smooth and elastic, about 5 minutes. Place dough in a lightly greased bowl. Cover and let dough rise in a warm place ½ hour.

Pat dough into a lightly greased 12-inch pizza pan or onto a lightly greased baking sheet. Press up edges to make a slight rim.

Fry bacon until crisp. Remove from grease and drain on absorbent paper. Add onions to bacon grease; cook slowly until tender but not brown. Sprinkle onion, bacon, cumin, ½ teaspoon salt, and pepper over dough. Bake at 400°F for 20 minutes.

Blend egg yolk and sour cream. Pour over onions. Bake for 10 to 15 minutes longer or until golden brown and sour cream is set.

Serve warm or at room temperature. Makes 8 servings.

farmer's breakfast

farmer's breakfast
bauernfrühstück

A good lunch or dinner dish. Serve with a green salad and bread.

4 medium potatoes
4 strips bacon, cubed
3 eggs
3 tablespoons milk
½ teaspoon salt
**1 cup cooked ham, cut into
  small cubes**
2 medium tomatoes, peeled
1 tablespoon chopped chives

Boil unpeeled potatoes 30 minutes. Rinse under cold water, peel, and set aside to cool. Slice potatoes.

In a large frypan cook bacon until transparent. Add the potato slices; cook until lightly browned.

Meanwhile blend eggs with milk and salt. Stir in the cubed ham.

Cut the tomatoes into thin wedges; add to the egg mixture. Pour the egg mixture over the potatoes in the frypan. Cook until the eggs are set.

Sprinkle with chopped chives and serve at once. Makes 3 to 4 servings.

baked spinach with cheese
überbackener spinat mit käse

1 pound fresh spinach,
   washed and dried
¼ pound butter
1 large onion, diced
2 cloves garlic, minced
½ teaspoon salt

½ pound Emmenthaler
   cheese, grated
1 teaspoon paprika
⅛ teaspoon nutmeg
¼ teaspoon pepper

Cut spinach into strips.

In a large Dutch oven heat butter until bubbly. Add onion and garlic; sauté for 2 to 3 minutes. Add the spinach. Sprinkle with salt. Cover and steam for 5 minutes. Remove from heat.

Grease an ovenproof casserole. Sprinkle half the cheese over the bottom of the casserole. Add the spinach. Sprinkle with paprika, nutmeg, and pepper. Top with remaining cheese. Bake at 350°F about 20 minutes or until cheese bubbles. Makes 4 servings.

stuffed cabbage rolls
gefüllt krautrouladen

1½ cups brown rice
3 cups water
2 teaspoons salt
1 teaspoon dillseed
½ teaspoon marjoram
¾ teaspoon pepper
2½ cups chopped onion
5 tablespoons vegetable oil
½ teaspoon paprika
2 cloves garlic, minced
2 eggs, lightly beaten

¼ cup bread crumbs
¼ cup minced fresh parsley
2½ pounds cabbage
Cheesecloth (about 6 feet)
2½ cups chopped canned
   tomatoes
½ cup dry vermouth
½ cup beef broth
2 tablespoons tomato paste
½ teaspoon sugar

In a medium bowl cover brown rice with hot water and soak for 3 hours. Drain.

In a 2-quart saucepan combine rice, 3 cups water, and 1½ teaspoons salt. Simmer covered for 40 minutes or until the liquid is absorbed. Add the dillseed, marjoram, and ½ teaspoon pepper.

In a large skillet sauté 1½ cups chopped onion in 3 tablespoons hot vegetable oil until soft, about 6 to 8 minutes. Add paprika and garlic; continue cooking and stirring for 2 minutes. Stir in the rice mixture, eggs, bread crumbs, and parsley. Adjust seasonings to taste.

Core the cabbage and, in a large pot, blanch the cabbage core-side-down in boiling salted water for 5 minutes or until it is softened. Drain. Remove 12 leaves and cut off one-fourth of each leaf from the base. Arrange 1 leaf curved-side-down on a square of dampened cheesecloth and place 3 tablespoons of the rice mixture in the center. Wrap the leaf around the filling and twist the corners of the cheesecloth to form the leaf into a roll. Continue making rolls with remaining filling.

Chop remaining cabbage to make 3 cups and, in a large frypan, sauté with 1 cup chopped onions and 2 tablespoons vegetable oil until soft. Add tomatoes, vermouth, broth, tomato paste, sugar, ½ teaspoon salt and ¼ teaspoon pepper. Simmer the mixture for 5 minutes, stirring occasionally. Adjust seasonings.

Transfer cabbage-tomato sauce mixture to a large baking dish. Arrange the cabbage rolls close together in one layer on the sauce. Spoon some of the mixture over the rolls. Bake at 325°F for 1½ hours. Baste rolls 4 to 5 times during cooking. Let the dish cool. Cover and refrigerate overnight.

Remove cheesecloth. Heat in a preheated 350°F oven for 30 minutes before serving. Makes 6 servings.

eggs in green sauce
eier in grüner sosse

This cold dish is perfect for summer dinners. Green sauce originated in Frankfurt and was Goethe's favorite dish.

In Germany, this dish is served with potatoes boiled in their skins. The potatoes are peeled at the table and dunked into the sauce.

2 tablespoons mayonnaise
1 cup sour cream (part yogurt can be used)
1 lemon, juiced
9 hard-cooked eggs
½ teaspoon salt
¼ teaspoon pepper
½ teaspoon sugar
1½ cups chopped fresh herbs (any combination of dill, chives, parsley, tarragon, or borage)

Blend mayonnaise, sour cream, and lemon juice.

Finely chop 1 hard-cooked egg and stir into mayonnaise mixture. Season with salt, pepper, and sugar.

Thoroughly rinse the herbs, pat dry, and chop. Blend with the sauce.

Slice rest of hard-cooked eggs in half and arrange in the sauce. Makes 4 servings.

grilled bratwurst
gegrillte bratwurst

6 bratwursts
1 can beer
1 medium onion, chopped
6 peppercorns
4 cloves
6 hard rolls

Place bratwursts, beer, onion, peppercorns, and cloves in a 3-quart saucepan. Simmer for 20 minutes. Drain.

Grill bratwursts 2 to 5 inches from charcoal about 10 minutes, until browned. Sprinkle with water to form crisp skin.

Serve in hard rolls with Dusseldorf-style mustard. Makes 6 servings.

hunter's stew
jäger-eintopf

1½ cups minced onions
¼ pound mushrooms, sliced
2 tablespoons vegetable oil
1 pound lean ground beef
1 cup beef broth
⅝ teaspoon nutmeg
½ teaspoon Worcestershire sauce
1 teaspoon salt
½ teaspoon pepper
3 medium potatoes
3 tablespoons butter
2 eggs
4 tart apples
½ cup fine dry bread crumbs

In a frypan sauté onions and mushrooms in vegetable oil until soft. Add ground beef; sauté mixture 3 to 4 minutes. Stir in broth; bring to a simmer. Add ½ teaspoon nutmeg, Worcestershire sauce, ½ teaspoon salt, and ¼ teaspoon pepper.

Peel the potatoes and boil them in salted water until tender, about 30 minutes. Drain, and put through a food mill or grinder. Beat in 2 tablespoons butter, ½ teaspoon salt, and ¼ teaspoon pepper. Adjust seasonings to taste. Beat in eggs and remaining nutmeg.

Peel, core and slice apples. Layer mixtures in a 1½-quart buttered baking dish. Spread ⅓ of potatoes on bottom of dish. Top with ½ of the meat mixture and ½ of the apples. Continue with layers, ending with a layer of potatoes. Sprinkle the top with bread crumbs, and dot with remaining butter. Bake at 375°F for 45 minutes and then at 400°F for 10 minutes more. Makes 4 servings.

meat, poultry, game, and fish

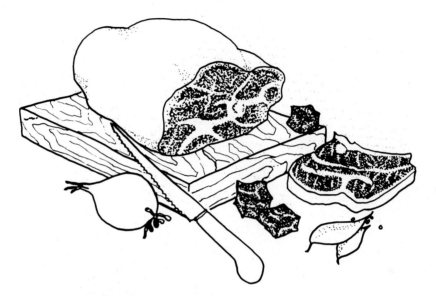

ragout a la berghoff
berghoff ragout

¾ cup butter
3½-pound boneless round
  steak, cut into thin strips
1 cup chopped onion
1½ cup chopped green pepper
1 pound mushrooms, sliced
½ cup flour
2 cups beef broth, canned or
  homemade
1 cup dry white wine
1 teaspoon salt
1 teaspoon Worcestershire
  sauce
Few drops Tabasco sauce (to
  taste)

Melt ½ cup butter in large frypan. Brown meat over medium-high heat.
Remove browned meat.

In remaining butter sauté onion for 2 minutes. Add green pepper and
mushrooms. Cook an additional 3 minutes.

Melt ¼ cup butter and add flour. Slowly add beef broth; cook until
thickened. Stir in wine and seasonings. Add meat and mushroom
mixture. Cover and simmer 45 minutes to 1 hour, until meat is tender.

Serve with buttered noodles or dumplings. Makes 8 servings.

bamberger meat and cabbage casserole

bamberger krautbraten

1 small head cabbage (about 1
  pound)
1 tablespoon vegetable oil
2 medium onions, chopped
½ pound lean pork, cubed
1 pound lean ground beef
1 teaspoon caraway seeds
½ teaspoon salt
½ teaspoon pepper
½ cup dry white wine
1 teaspoon vegetable oil
3 to 6 strips thickly sliced
  bacon

Remove outer, wilted cabbage leaves and core. Place cabbage in a large pot of boiling water and simmer gently for 10 minutes. Remove and drain. Gently pull off 12 leaves and set aside. Finely chop the rest of the cabbage.

Heat 1 tablespoon vegetable oil; add onions, pork and ground beef. Cook until lightly browned. Drain off excess fat. Add the chopped cabbage, caraway seeds, salt, and pepper. Pour in the white wine. Cover and simmer the mixture for 10 minutes, stirring often.

Grease an ovenproof dish with 1 teaspoon of vegetable oil; line the dish with half the cabbage leaves. Spoon in the meat mixture; cover with the rest of the cabbage leaves.

Cut bacon strips in half and arrange on top. Place in preheated 350°F oven; bake for approximately 45 minutes. Makes 4 servings.

beef goulash

rindergulasch

3 tablespoons vegetable oil
1 pound round steak, cubed
3 medium onions, chopped
½ teaspoon salt
¼ teaspoon pepper
½ teaspoon garlic salt
1 teaspoon paprika
¼ teaspoon sugar
2 cups hot water
1 tablespoon flour
¼ cup cold water
½ cup heavy cream

Heat vegetable oil in a large frypan or Dutch oven. Add meat cubes and brown well, approximately 10 minutes. Stir in onions; cook until soft. Sprinkle with salt, pepper, garlic salt, paprika, and sugar. Blend thoroughly. Pour in hot water; cover and simmer gently about 1½ hours.

In a small jar or container shake or blend flour with cold water. Be sure to break up all lumps. Add to meat about 7 minutes before the end of cooking time. Stir constantly until sauce is thickened and bubbling. Remove from heat; stir in cream.

Serve with noodles, accompanied by a tomato salad if desired. Makes 4 servings.

Picture on opposite page: bamberger meat and cabbage casserole

beef rolls

beef rolls
rinderrouladen

The people of Berlin claim the origin of this dish.

4 pieces steak roll or sandwich steaks, each about 6 ounces	2 ounces salt pork (or 2 strips bacon), cut into thin strips
2 teaspoons Dijon-style mustard	1 large onion, chopped
½ teaspoon salt	¼ cup vegetable oil
¼ teaspoon pepper	1½ cups hot beef broth
2 large pickles, cut into long, thin strips	4 peppercorns
	½ bay leaf
	1 tablespoon cornstarch

Divide pickles, salt pork (or bacon), and onion among the steaks.

Lay steaks on a flat surface. Spread each with mustard; sprinkle with salt and pepper.

Divide pickles, salt pork (or bacon), and onion among the steaks as shown. Roll up steaks jelly-roll fashion; secure with beef-roll clamps, toothpicks, or thread.

Heat oil in a heavy saucepan, add the steak rolls, and brown well on all sides, about 15 minutes. Pour in hot beef broth, peppercorns, and bay leaf. Cover and simmer for 1 hour and 20 minutes. Remove beef rolls, discard clamps, and arrange on a preheated platter.

Blend cornstarch with a small amount of cold water, stir into gravy, and bring to a boil, until thick and bubbly. Correct seasonings and serve separately. Makes 4 servings.

sauerbraten

4 pounds boneless beef roast
1 cup water
1 cup wine vinegar
2 onions, sliced
1 teaspoon salt
6 peppercorns
2 bay leaves

2 cloves
2 tablespoons vegetable oil
1 medium tomato, peeled and
 chopped
2 tablespoons flour
2 teaspoons sugar
¼ cup water

Place meat in a large container (not metal).

In a saucepan bring water, vinegar, onions, salt, peppercorns, bay leaves, and cloves to a boil. Simmer for 10 minutes. Cool marinade to room temperature. Pour marinade over meat. Refrigerate for 2 to 3 days, turning several times each day.

Remove meat from marinade, and dry. Brown meat in hot vegetable oil in a Dutch oven. Add the tomato and marinade liquid. Cover and simmer gently 1 to 2 hours, until meat is tender.

The meat could also be placed in a 325°F oven and baked, or it could be cooked on low in a slow cooker 3 to 4 hours.

Remove meat from juices. Also remove peppercorns, cloves, and bay leaves.

Mix flour and sugar with water until lumps disappear. Add to pan juices and cook until thickened.

Serve with boiled potatoes and red cabbage. Makes 6 to 8 servings.

sauerbraten with gingersnap gravy
sauerbraten mit ingwer kuchen sosse

4-pound beef rump roast
2 onions, thinly sliced
8 peppercorns
4 cloves
1 bay leaf
1 cup mild white vinegar
1 cup water

½ cup cider vinegar
¼ cup vegetable oil
½ teaspoon salt
2 cups boiling water
10 gingersnaps
½ cup sour cream
1 tablespoon flour

Place the beef roast in a deep ceramic or glass bowl. Add onions, peppercorns, cloves, and bay leaf. Pour white vinegar, water, and cider vinegar over the meat; chill, covered, for 4 days. Turn meat twice each day.

Remove the meat from the marinade, dry it well with paper towels, and strain the marinade into a bowl. Reserve the onions and 1 cup of marinade.

In a Dutch oven brown the meat on all sides in hot vegetable oil. Sprinkle meat with salt. Pour boiling water around the meat, sprinkle in crushed gingersnaps, and simmer, covered, for 1½ hours. Turn often. Add 1 cup of reserved marinade and cook meat 2 hours or more, until tender.

Remove the meat and keep it warm. Strain the cooking juices into a large saucepan.

In a small bowl mix sour cream with flour. Stir it into the cooking juices and cook, stirring, until sauce is thickened and smooth. Slice the meat in ¼-inch slices; add to the hot gravy.

Arrange meat on a heated platter and pour extra sauce over it. Makes 8 to 10 servings.

beef roast with mushroom stuffing

rostbraten mit pilzfülle

½ teaspoon salt
¼ teaspoon white pepper
2 pounds flank steak
1 teaspoon Dijon-style
   mustard

mushroom stuffing
2 tablespoons vegetable oil
1 small onion, chopped
4-ounce can mushroom pieces,
   drained and chopped
¼ cup chopped parsley
2 tablespoons chopped chives
1 tablespoon tomato paste
¼ cup dried bread crumbs
¼ teaspoon salt
¼ teaspoon pepper
1 teaspoon paprika

gravy
3 strips bacon, cubed
2 small onions, finely chopped
1 cup hot beef broth
1 teaspoon Dijon-style
   mustard
2 tablespoons tomato catsup

Lightly salt and pepper flank steak on both sides. Spread one side with mustard.

To prepare stuffing, heat vegetable oil in a frypan, add onion, and cook for 3 minutes, until lightly browned. Add mushroom pieces; cook for 5 minutes. Stir in parsley, chives, tomato paste, and bread crumbs. Season with salt, pepper, and paprika.

Spread stuffing on mustard side of flank steak, roll up jelly-roll fashion, and tie with thread or string.

To prepare gravy, cook bacon in a Dutch oven until partially done. Add the meat roll and brown on all sides, approximately 10 minutes. Add the onions and sauté for 5 minutes. Pour in beef broth, cover Dutch oven, and simmer for 1 hour. Remove meat to a preheated platter. Season pan juices with mustard. Salt and pepper to taste; stir in catsup.

Serve the gravy separately. Makes 6 servings.

beef stew

rindfleisch-eintopf

¼ cup shortening
3-pound boneless rump roast
2 cups sliced onions
¼ cup flour
2 tablespoons salt
2 tablespoons sugar

Pepper to taste
2 teaspoons dry mustard
½ teaspoon celery seed
¼ cup water
1 1-pound can tomatoes

Melt shortening in a Dutch oven. Add the meat and brown on all sides. Place the onions on top of the meat.

Mix the flour and seasonings with ¼ cup water. Blend with the tomatoes and add the mixture to the Dutch oven. Bake at 325°F about 2 hours, until meat is fork-tender.

Serve with oven-browned potatoes. Makes 6 servings.

Picture on opposite page:
beef roast with mushroom stuffing

german meatloaf
falscher hase

This German title actually means false rabbit. Although each housewife has her own version of the false rabbit, this one is quite typical.

½ pound lean ground beef
½ pound lean ground pork
1 medium onion, chopped
3 tablespoons bread crumbs
3 tablespoons cold water
2 eggs
½ teaspoon salt
1 teaspoon paprika
1 teaspoon prepared mustard
2 tablespoons chopped parsley

3 hard-cooked eggs, peeled
4 strips bacon
4 tablespoons vegetable oil
1 cup beef broth
sauce
¼ cup hot water
1 teaspoon cornstarch
¼ cup water
½ cup sour cream

Thoroughly mix ground meats, onion, bread crumbs, 3 tablespoons cold water, and eggs. Flavor with salt, paprika, mustard, and parsley. Blend ingredients thoroughly. Flatten out meat mixture in the shape of a square (8 by 8 inches). Arrange whole hard-boiled eggs in a row along the middle of the meat. Fold sides of meat pattie over the eggs. Shape meat carefully into a loaf resembling a flat bread loaf. Occasionally rinse hands in cold water to prevent sticking.

Cube 2 strips bacon; cook in a Dutch oven about 2 minutes. Carefully add the vegetable oil; heat. Place meatloaf in the Dutch oven and cook until browned on all sides. Cut remaining bacon strips in half and arrange over the top of the meatloaf. Place uncovered Dutch oven in a preheated 350°F oven for about 45 minutes. While meat is baking, gradually pour hot beef broth over the top of the meatloaf; brush occasionally with pan drippings. When done, remove meat to a preheated platter and keep it warm.

Add ¼ cup of hot water to pan and scrape all particles from the bottom. Bring to a gentle boil and add cornstarch that has been mixed with ¼ cup water. Cook until bubbly and thick. Remove from heat and stir in sour cream. Reheat to warm. Season with salt and pepper if desired. Serve the sauce separately. Makes 4 servings.

meatloaf with cauliflower
hackbraten mit blumenkohl

1 pound ground beef
1 egg
¼ cup milk
⅓ cup dry bread crumbs
½ cup chopped onion
½ teaspoon salt
1 teaspoon Worcestershire
  sauce
¼ teaspoon pepper
1 small head cauliflower
1 cup grated sharp cheddar
  cheese
1 cup evaporated milk
3 tomatoes, halved

Mix beef, egg, milk, crumbs, onion, and seasonings to make a meatloaf. Mold into ring in 2-quart round baking dish.

Parboil cauliflower 5 minutes. Place in center of meatloaf.

Mix cheese and milk; pour over cauliflower.

Bake at 350°F for 45 minutes to 1 hour. Last 5 minutes of baking, place tomatoes on top of meatloaf. Makes 4 servings.

steaks esterhazy

¼ pound mushrooms, diced
1 small carrot, diced
1 shallot or green onion, minced
2 tablespoons butter
1 teaspoon paprika
½ teaspoon salt
1 cup sour cream
1 teaspoon Worcestershire sauce
4 servings beef sirloin, T-bone, or fillet steaks

Sauté mushrooms, carrot, and shallot or green onion in butter. Add paprika, salt, sour cream, and Worcestershire sauce. Simmer for 2 minutes but do not boil.

Broil steaks and top with sauce. Makes 4 servings.

german beefsteaks
deutsches beefsteak

1 large, dry hard roll
½ cup water
4 tablespoons vegetable oil
1 medium onion, chopped
1 pound lean ground beef
½ teaspoon salt
¼ teaspoon pepper
4 medium onions, sliced

In a small bowl soak roll in water.

Heat 2 tablespoons vegetable oil in a frypan; cook chopped onion until lightly browned. Transfer onion to a bowl.

Squeeze roll as dry as possible and mix roll with onions. Add ground beef; blend well. Season with salt and pepper. Shape meat into 4 patties.

Heat 2 tablespoons vegetable oil in a frypan. Add ground-beef patties; cook about 5 minutes on each side or to desired doneness. Remove and keep warm.

Add sliced onions to pan drippings; cook until lightly browned.

Arrange beefsteaks on a platter and top with onion rings. Makes 4 servings.

beef strips and carrots
möhren mit geschnetzeltern

1 pound carrots
⅔ cup carbonated soda water
1 cup white wine
1 teaspoon salt
¼ teaspoon sugar
1 pound sirloin steak
2 tablespoons vegetable oil
2 small onions, diced
¼ teaspoon white pepper
½ cup heavy cream
1 tablespoon chopped parsley

Peel carrots and cut into thin slices (crosswise at a slant). Place in a saucepan with the soda water, wine, ½ teaspoon salt, and sugar. Cover and simmer for 25 minutes or until tender.

Meanwhile cut the meat into very thin slices.

Heat the vegetable oil and sauté the onions about 5 minutes. Add the beef slices; cook for 5 minutes, stirring often. Season with ½ teaspoon salt and ¼ teaspoon pepper. Add the meat and onions to the carrots. Mix carefully. Stir in the cream. Heat through but do not boil. Correct seasonings if necessary.

Sprinkle with chopped parsley and serve. Makes 4 servings.

sauerbraten meatballs
sauerbraten klopse

1 pound lean ground beef
¼ cup milk
¼ cup dry bread crumbs
⅛ teaspoon ground cloves
⅛ teaspoon ground allspice
½ teaspoon salt
Pepper to taste
2 tablespoons vegetable oil
1 cup plus 2 tablespoons water
½ cup vinegar
¾ teaspoon ground ginger
1 bay leaf
4 tablespoons brown sugar
2 tablespoons flour

Mix beef, milk, crumbs, cloves, allspice, salt, and pepper. Form into meatballs. Brown meatballs in hot oil. Drain off fat. Add 1 cup water, vinegar, ginger, bay leaf and brown sugar. Cover and simmer ½ hour. Skim off fat. Remove meatballs and keep them warm.

Mix flour and 2 tablespoons water. Slowly stir into the pan juices to make gravy. Pour gravy over meatballs.

Serve with buttered noodles. Makes 4 servings.

meatballs königsberg-style
königsberger klopse

meatballs
1 roll
¾ cup water
1 pound lean ground beef
1 strip bacon, diced
4 anchovy fillets, diced
1 small onion, chopped
1 egg
½ teaspoon salt
¼ teaspoon white pepper

broth
6 cups water
½ teaspoon salt
1 bay leaf
1 small onion, peeled and
   halved
6 peppercorns

gravy
1½ tablespoons butter or
   margarine
1½ tablespoons flour
1 tablespoon capers
Juice of ½ lemon
½ teaspoon prepared mustard
1 egg yolk
¼ teaspoon salt
¼ teaspoon white pepper

Soak the roll in the water for about 10 minutes. Squeeze it dry; place in mixing bowl with the ground beef. Add the bacon, anchovy fillets, onion, egg, salt, and pepper. Mix thoroughly.

Prepare the broth by boiling the water, seasoned with salt, bay leaf, onion, and peppercorns.

Shape the meat mixture into balls about 2 inches in diameter. Add to the boiling broth and simmer over low heat for 20 minutes. Remove meatballs with a slotted spoon, set aside, and keep warm. Strain the broth through a sieve. Reserve broth and keep warm.

To prepare gravy, heat butter in a frypan and stir in flour. Cook for 3 minutes, stirring constantly. Slowly blend in 2 cups of reserved broth. Add the drained capers, lemon juice, and mustard. Simmer for 5 minutes. Remove a small amount of the sauce to blend with the egg yolk. Stir egg yolk back into the sauce. Season with salt and pepper.

Place reserved meatballs into the gravy and reheat if necessary. Serve on a preheated platter. Makes 4 servings.

Picture on opposite page: meatballs königsberg-style

stuffed cabbage
krautrouladen

12 outer leaves from cabbage
8 strips bacon
1 medium onion, chopped
¾ pound ground beef
2 cups cooked rice
Pinch paprika
½ teaspoon salt
¼ teaspoon pepper
1-pound can sauerkraut, drained
1 8-ounce can tomato sauce
½ can undiluted tomato soup
2 teaspoons sugar

Blanch cabbage leaves in boiling water 5 minutes.

In a frypan sauté 4 strips of bacon and the onion until bacon is crisp.

Mix ground meat, rice, and seasonings with bacon and onion. Place 2 tablespoons filling on each cabbage leaf. Roll up, folding in ends, and secure with toothpicks.

Place sauerkraut in bottom of a 2-quart casserole. Place cabbage rolls on top of sauerkraut.

Mix tomato sauce and soup and pour over cabbage rolls. Lay remaining 4 strips of bacon over top. Sprinkle with sugar. Cover casserole and bake 1 hour in preheated 325°F oven. If sauce is too thin, uncover last ½ hour of baking. Makes 6 servings.

roast pork with madeira sauce
schweinebraten mit madeirasosse

3 to 4-pound pork roast, boneless
Peel from 1 lemon
2 bay leaves
½ teaspoon salt
⅛ teaspoon white pepper
1 tablespoon vinegar
1 cup dry white wine
2 tablespoons flour
¼ cup Madeira wine

Place roast in roasting pan. Place lemon peel and bay leaves in bottom of pan.

Mix salt, pepper, vinegar, and white wine. Pour over meat. Roast meat at 325°F until internal temperature reaches 170°F (about 2 to 2½ hours). Baste meat with pan juices about every ½ hour. When roast is done, remove from pan. Degrease pan juice.

Mix flour with Madeira wine; gradually add to juices, stirring constantly with wire whisk. Cook until gravy thickens.

Slice meat and serve with gravy and spaetzle, potatoes, or noodles. Makes 6 to 8 servings.

hunter's stew with cabbage
jäger-eintopf mit kohl

Although of Polish origin, this stew is still served today in Germany on days of the Hunt. This stew is good if prepared ahead and reheated.

6 cups thinly sliced cabbage (about 2 pounds)
1 1-pound, 12-ounce can sauerkraut
1½ teaspoon salt
2 bay leaves
8 pork loin chops
1½ cups water
1 pound smoked sausage or frankfurters, sliced ½ inch thick
2 8-ounce cans tomato sauce

Spread cabbage in the bottom of a large roaster. Cover with sauerkraut. Sprinkle with salt. Add bay leaves. Place pork chops on top and add water. Cover and bake at 325°F for 1 hour. Add sausage and tomato sauce. Continue baking until meat is tender.

Serve with boiled potatoes. Makes 8 servings.

pork chop and rice casserole

pork chop and rice casserole

reis mit schnitzeln überbacken

tomato sauce
¼ cup vegetable oil
3 medium ripe tomatoes, sliced
2 medium onions, chopped
2 garlic cloves, minced
½ teaspoon salt
¼ teaspoon white pepper
¼ teaspoon dried oregano leaves

rice
1 cup uncooked long-grain rice
Water and salt (according to package directions)

chops
4 pork chops
½ teaspoon salt
¼ teaspoon white pepper
¼ teaspoon paprika
2 tablespoons vegetable oil
Margarine to grease casserole
3 tablespoons grated Emmenthal or Swiss cheese
1 tablespoon butter

To prepare sauce, heat vegetable oil in a frypan; sauté tomato slices, onions, and garlic for about 5 minutes, stirring constantly. Season with salt, pepper, and oregano. Cover and simmer tomatoes in their own juices for about 20 minutes. Strain through a sieve and return puree to the frypan. Cook until liquid is reduced to two-thirds, stirring frequently. Set aside.

Meanwhile, prepare rice according to package directions. Set aside.

Season pork chops with salt, pepper, and paprika. Heat oil in a frypan, add chops, and fry for 5 minutes on each side.

Generously grease an ovenproof dish. Cover bottom with half the rice and pour half the tomato sauce over the rice. Arrange 2 pork chops on top, and sprinkle with half the grated cheese. Repeat layers. Dot with butter. Place in a preheated 350°F oven; bake for 30 to 40 minutes. Makes 4 servings.

pork chops in onion sauce

pork chops in onion sauce

schweinekotelett in zwiebelsosse

4 pork chops	4 small (or 2 medium) onions,
½ teaspoon salt	thinly sliced
¼ teaspoon pepper	½ cup beer
1½ tablespoons flour	½ cup hot beef broth
1½ tablespoons vegetable oil	1 teaspoon cornstarch

Season pork chops with salt and pepper; coat with flour. Heat oil in a heavy frypan. Add pork chops; fry for 3 minutes on each side. Add onions; cook for another 5 minutes, turning chops once. Pour in beer and beef broth; cover and simmer for 15 minutes. Remove pork chops to a preheated platter. Season sauce to taste.

Blend cornstarch with a small amount of cold water. Stir into sauce and cook until thick and bubbly. Pour over pork chops.

Serve with brussel sprouts and boiled potatoes. Makes 4 servings.

baked pork chops

schweinekoteletts in saurer sahnesosse

6 pork chops	½ teaspoon salt
1 clove garlic, minced	Pepper as desired
1 teaspoon crushed caraway	1 cup dry white wine
seeds	1 cup sour cream (optional)
2 teaspoons mild Hungarian	
paprika (available at	
gourmet and specialty	
stores)	

Place the pork chops in an ovenproof casserole.

Mix the remaining ingredients, except sour cream, and pour over the chops. Marinate the chops 2 to 3 hours in the refrigerator.

Bake the chops, uncovered, in the marinade in a preheated 325°F oven for 1 hour or until tender. Add more wine if needed. Stir sour cream into pan juices and heat through but do not boil.

Serve chops with sour-cream gravy and buttered noodles or dumplings. Makes 6 servings.

pork chops
dusseldorf
schweinekoteletts düsseldorf

8 pork chops
2 tablespoons vegetable oil
½ cup chopped onion
1 cup dry white wine
1½ tablespoons
    Dusseldorf-style mustard
1¼ cups canned beef broth
2 tablespoons cornstarch
4 small sour gherkins, cut in
    half

In a large frypan brown the chops in hot oil. Remove the browned chops; sauté the onion until transparent. Carefully pour in the wine; stir to remove the browned particles.

Mix the mustard with the beef broth.

Place the chops in the pan with the onion mixture; pour 1 cup beef broth over top. Cover and bake in a preheated 325°F oven 30 to 45 minutes, until tender. Remove chops to a heated platter. Keep them warm.

Mix the cornstarch with remaining ¼ cup beef broth. Blend into the juices to make gravy. Heat until thick and bubbly.

Pour gravy over the meat; garnish with sliced gherkins. Makes 4 servings.

stuffed
pork chops
gefüllte schweineschnitzel

6 slices boiled ham
6 slices Swiss cheese
12 boneless pork chops,
    pounded ¼-inch thick
1 cup milk

1 cup flour
3 eggs, beaten
1½ cups dry bread crumbs
¼ cup vegetable oil

Place 1 slice of ham and 1 slice of cheese between two slices of pork. (Pound pork as thin as possible.) Secure with toothpicks or string. Dip each in milk, then in flour. Shake off excess flour; dip into eggs, then into crumbs. Place in refrigerator at least ½ hour to dry coating.

Brown chops in hot oil in ovenproof frypan or covered casserole. Place in 350°F oven and bake, covered, about 30 minutes, until done.

If chops are very thin, they can be fried in oil, about 5 to 8 minutes on each side, and served immediately. Makes 6 servings.

pork ribs
and sauerkraut
schweinerippchen und
sauerkraut

1-pound, 12-ounce can
    sauerkraut
1 cup chopped onion
1-pound, 12-ounce can
    tomatoes
¾ cup firmly packed brown
    sugar
3 pounds country-style pork
    ribs

Layer ingredients in a large casserole or roaster as listed, starting with sauerkraut and ending with ribs. Do not stir. Cover and bake at 325°F for 3 hours. Uncover last 45 minutes of baking. Makes 6 servings.

spareribs and sauerkraut

hochrippe und sauerkraut

2 16-ounce cans sauerkraut
3 pounds country-style
  spareribs
2 teaspoons paprika

6 bouillon cubes
½ teaspoon caraway seeds
½ teaspoon pepper
10 slices bacon, rolled in flour

Rinse and drain the sauerkraut. Place sauerkraut in large 4- or 6-quart casserole. Add 2 quarts hot water. Add uncooked spareribs, paprika, bouillon cubes, caraway seeds, and pepper. Cook, covered, over low heat 3 to 4 hours.

Fry floured bacon slices. Break bacon into sauerkraut. Remove bones from the sauce before serving.

Serve with dark bread and steins of beer. Makes 4 to 6 servings.

bavarian veal

schwalbennester

1 pound veal, cut into 4 thin
  slices
½ teaspoon salt
⅛ teaspoon sugar
½ teaspoon white pepper
1 tablespoon Dijon mustard
4 slices bacon

4 hard-cooked eggs
2 tablespoons vegetable oil
1 onion, diced
¾ cup beef bouillon, heated
1 tablespoon tomato paste
2 tablespoons flour
¼ cup red wine

Dry veal on paper towels. Roll in a mixture of salt, sugar, white pepper, and mustard. Place a bacon slice on top of each piece of veal. Place an unsliced egg on top of the bacon. Roll up each slice of veal (jelly-roll fashion) and tie together with string.

Heat oil in a frypan and brown veal rolls well on all sides. Add onion; sauté for 3 minutes. Add the hot bouillon; cover and simmer gently 25 minutes. Remove the veal from the pan. Remove the strings from the veal and keep veal warm on a serving platter.

Add tomato paste to the pan drippings; stir.

Thoroughly mix flour and red wine to remove all lumps. Add to sauce and cook until mixture thickens. Add warm veal rolls and heat through.

Before serving, place veal rolls on a platter, pour sauce over the rolls, and serve with pureed potatoes, if desired. Makes 4 servings.

bavarian veal with asparagus

bayerischer mit spargel

2 pounds veal cubes
2 tablespoons vegetable oil
1 large onion, chopped
1 cup chopped carrots
1 tablespoon chopped parsley
¼ cup fresh lemon juice
2 cups beef broth
3 tablespoons flour

½ teaspoon salt
Freshly ground pepper to
  taste
2 10-ounce boxes frozen
  asparagus tips and pieces
  or 2 pounds fresh, cleaned
  and cut into 1-inch pieces

In a Dutch oven brown the veal in hot oil. Add onion and carrots. Cook until onion is transparent. Stir in parsley.

Mix lemon juice, broth, flour, and seasonings until well-blended. Pour over meat. Cover and bake in preheated 325°F oven 1½ hours or until meat is tender. Add more broth, if needed.

Cook asparagus until tender-crisp. Stir into veal and serve immediately. Makes 6 servings.

veal steaks with lemon and curry
kalbsschnitzel in currysosse

1 pound veal cutlets, sliced
   thin
½ teaspoon salt
¼ teaspoon pepper
¾ teaspoon curry powder
3 tablespoons vegetable oil
2 onions, diced
2 tablespoons evaporated milk
2 tablespoons tomato paste
1 lemon, juiced
10 sprigs parsley, chopped
2 tablespoons cognac or
   brandy

Season veal with salt, pepper, and ½ teaspoon curry.

Heat oil; brown veal slices on both sides. Remove meat and reserve. Add onions; sauté until softened. Add evaporated milk and tomato paste. Cook until bubbly. Add lemon juice, rest of curry, and chopped parsley. Return the veal slices to the sauce. Add the cognac or brandy; heat through.

Serve on a warmed platter. Makes 4 servings.

veal steaks with yogurt
kalbsschnitzel mit joghurt

1 pound veal, sliced thin
½ teaspoon salt
¼ teaspoon pepper
3 tablespoons vegetable oil
3 to 4 medium apples, peeled
   and sliced
½ cup evaporated milk
1 small container yogurt

Rub veal steaks with salt and pepper.

Heat oil and cook veal slices about 2 minutes on each side. Place veal in an ovenproof casserole. Add apples.

Blend evaporated milk and yogurt together. Spread over apples. Place in a preheated 325°F oven; cook just until bubbly, about 20 to 30 minutes. Makes 4 servings.

veal rounds with vegetables
kalbsschnitzel mit feinen gemüsen

Salt to taste (about ½
   teaspoon)
Pepper to taste (about ¼
   teaspoon)
Paprika to taste (about ¼
   teaspoon)
4 veal fillets, cut ¼ inch thick

4 tablespoons butter
4 whole stewed tomatoes
12 canned white asparagus
   spears
¼ pound fresh mushrooms,
   sliced

Sprinkle salt, pepper, and paprika over the veal slices. Sauté in butter until browned. On each fillet place 1 stewed tomato, 3 spears asparagus, and a heaping tablespoon mushrooms. Cook gently. Pour cooking juices over the fillets while cooking. Cook, uncovered, until mushrooms are just tender.

Serve with pureed potatoes and a salad. Makes 4 servings.

stuffed veal breast
gefüllte kalbsbrust

½ pound lean ground beef
¼ pound ground pork
1 egg
1 cup soft bread crumbs
1 tablespoon lemon juice
⅛ teaspoon nutmeg
½ teaspoon salt
Pepper to taste
4-pound breast of veal with
   brisket on

3 tablespoons shortening
2 teaspoons paprika
2 bay leaves
6 cloves
½ teaspoon rosemary
½ teaspoon basil
2 cups water

Mix ground meats, egg, bread crumbs, lemon juice, nutmeg, salt, and pepper for stuffing. Stuff pocket of veal breast. Sew closed or use toothpicks or skewers. Brown roast in melted shortening in ovenproof casserole. To the drippings add paprika, bay leaves, cloves, rosemary, basil, and 2 cups water. Bake in a covered casserole at 325°F for 2 hours or until veal is tender.

Slice veal and serve immediately. Makes 4 servings.

veal breast with herb stuffing
kalbsbrust mit kräuterfüllung

herb stuffing
3 strips bacon
1 medium onion
1 4-ounce can mushroom
   pieces
¼ cup chopped fresh parsley
1 tablespoon chopped fresh
   dill
1 teaspoon dried tarragon
   leaves
1 teaspoon dried basil leaves
½ pound lean ground beef
½ cup dried bread crumbs

3 eggs
⅓ cup sour cream
½ teaspoon salt
¼ teaspoon pepper
veal
3 to 4 pounds boned veal
   breast or boned leg
½ teaspoon salt
¼ teaspoon pepper
1 tablespoon vegetable oil
2 cups hot beef broth
2 tablespoons cornstarch
½ cup sour cream

To prepare stuffing, dice bacon and onion. Cook bacon in a frypan until partially cooked; add onion and cook for 5 minutes. Drain and chop mushrooms, add to frypan, and cook for another 5 minutes. Remove mixture from heat, let cool, and transfer to a mixing bowl. Add herbs, ground beef, bread crumbs, eggs, and sour cream. Mix thoroughly. Season with salt and pepper.

With a sharp knife, cut a pocket in the veal breast or leg. Fill with stuffing; close opening with toothpicks. (Tie with string if necessary.) Rub outside with salt and pepper.

Heat oil in a Dutch oven. Place meat in the pan and bake in a preheated 350°F oven about 1½ hours. Baste occasionally with beef broth. When done, place meat on a preheated platter.

Pour rest of beef broth into the Dutch oven and scrape brown particles from the bottom. Bring pan drippings to a simmer. Thoroughly blend cornstarch with sour cream and add to pan drippings while stirring. Cook and stir until thick and bubbly.

Slice veal breast and serve sauce separately. Makes 6 servings.

veal cutlets
with capers
kapernschnitzel

**4 lean veal cutlets, about 6
  ounces each
2 tablespoons lemon juice
½ teaspoon salt
⅛ teaspoon pepper
½ teaspoon paprika
1 tablespoon vegetable oil
½ small jar capers, drained
¼ cup dry white wine
1 bay leaf
3 tablespoons evaporated milk
Sliced pickled beets for
  garnish
4 lettuce leaves for garnish**

Sprinkle cutlets with lemon juice and season with salt, pepper, and paprika.

Heat oil in a frypan and fry cutlets for 3 minutes on the first side. Turn cutlets over and add drained capers to pan. Fry again for 3 minutes; remove cutlets and arrange on a preheated platter.

Pour wine into pan, scraping loose any brown particles from bottom of frypan. Add bay leaf; simmer liquid 3 minutes. Remove bay leaf. Blend in evaporated milk and adjust seasonings.

Pour sauce over cutlets. Cut beets into strips and arrange on lettuce leaves as a garnish. Makes 4 servings.

veal cutlets with capers

veal cutlets with cherry sauce

veal cutlets with cherry sauce
kirsch-schnitzel

4 lean veal cutlets, about 6
   ounces each
1 tablespoon vegetable oil
½ teaspoon salt
⅛ teaspoon white pepper
¼ cup red wine
2 tablespoons evaporated milk
1 16-ounce can tart cherries,
   drained
Parsley for garnish

Pat cutlets dry with paper towels. Heat oil in a frypan and brown cutlets
on each side approximately 3 minutes. Season with salt and pepper.
Remove cutlets from pan and keep them warm.

Blend wine and evaporated milk in pan and simmer for 3 minutes. Add
cherries; heat through and adjust seasonings. Return cutlets to sauce and
reheat, but do not boil.

Arrange cutlets on preheated platter, pouring cherry sauce around them.
Garnish with parsley. Makes 4 servings.

blue
trout
forelle blau

4 ¾-pound freshwater trout
   (eviscerated only)
2 teaspoons salt
1 cup vinegar, heated
4 cups water
¼ cup white wine
1 sprig parsley for garnish
1 lemon for garnish
1 tomato for garnish

Rinse fish thoroughly with cold water. Sprinkle ¼ teaspoon salt inside each fish. To make the trout look attractive, tie a thread through the tail and the underside of the mouth to form a ring (see picture). Arrange fish on a large platter and pour hot vinegar over them. This process will turn them blue in color.

In a 4-quart saucepot bring water, remaining salt, and wine to a simmer. Carefully place the trout in the water and simmer (be sure not to boil) about 15 minutes. Remove trout with a slotted spoon, drain on paper towels, and arrange on a preheated platter. Garnish with parsley, lemon, and tomato slices. Makes 4 servings.

In Germany, fresh water trout is served with small boiled potatoes that have been tossed in melted butter and sprinkled with chopped parsley. A cold sauce accompanies the dish. This is made from 1 cup whipped heavy cream, ¼ teaspoon sugar, 2 tablespoons prepared horseradish, 1 teaspoon lemon juice, and salt and pepper to taste.

Tie a thread through the trout's tail and the underside of the mouth to form a ring.

blue trout

marinated rabbit
eingelegter hase

1 3-pound rabbit, cut into
    serving pieces
1 teaspoon salt
¼ teaspoon pepper
3 tablespoons vegetable oil

marinade
2 cups red wine
2 cups chicken broth
1 teaspoon allspice
2 bay leaves
1 teaspoon thyme

sauce
1 dozen pickled white onions
    (cocktail size)
1 dozen stuffed green olives,
    sliced
½ pound fresh mushrooms,
    sliced
2 tablespoons butter or
    margarine

Rub rabbit with salt and pepper; put into a large bowl.

Mix together marinade ingredients, add to rabbit, and refrigerate overnight.

Drain the pieces of rabbit, but do not pat dry. Strain and reserve the marinade.

In a large frypan over high heat, quickly brown all sides of rabbit pieces in hot vegetable oil. When brown, pour in reserved marinade and simmer over low heat 1 hour or until rabbit is tender.

Just before rabbit is done, sauté onions, olives, and mushrooms in hot butter or margarine. Add to rabbit mixture.

Serve with boiled potatoes. Makes 6 servings.

black forest stew
schwarzwald-eintopf

marinade
1 cup chopped onions
½ cup chopped carrot
½ cup chopped celery
1 clove garlic, minced
2 whole cloves
¼ teaspoon rosemary
¼ teaspoon thyme
1 bay leaf
6 cranberries
5 peppercorns
1 tablespoon chopped parsley
½ teaspoon salt
3 cups dry red wine
¼ cup red wine vinegar
½ cup vegetable oil

stew
3 pounds venison stew meat
½ teaspoon marjoram
¼ cup butter or margarine
1 cup chopped onions
¼ cup flour
1 cup beef broth
¼ teaspoon pepper
1 cup sour cream

Place marinade ingredients into a 2-quart saucepan. Bring marinade to a boil. Reduce heat and simmer 10 minutes. Cool.

Place venison and marjoram in a large casserole. Pour cooled marinade over meat. Cover and refrigerate for 24 hours, stirring occasionally.

Drain meat, reserving marinade. Pat meat dry.

In a large saucepan melt the butter. When hot, add the meat; brown, stirring to prevent burning. Remove meat and brown remaining 1 cup onions. Stir in flour; mix until well-blended. Add broth and 2 cups reserved marinade. Add pepper. Bring stew to a boil, stirring until slightly thickened. Add meat, cover, and simmer about 1 hour, until meat is tender. Skim off fat. Add sour cream and heat through. Makes 8 servings.

grandma's chicken
hähnchen auf grossmutter art

2 very small chickens
¼ cup vegetable oil
1 teaspoon salt
½ teaspoon white pepper
2 teaspoons paprika
6 medium potatoes
4 slices bacon
4 to 6 small onions
¼ cup hot beef bouillon
Parsley sprigs for garnish

Clean chickens.

Heat oil in a large Dutch oven. Add chickens; brown well on all sides for about 10 minutes. Season with salt, white pepper, and paprika. Continue cooking for another 10 minutes, turning often.

Meanwhile, peel potatoes and cut into 1-inch cubes.

Cut bacon into 1-inch pieces.

Add potatoes and bacon to chicken. Cook for 5 minutes.

Dice onions and stir in with hot beef bouillon. Cover and bake in a preheated 350°F oven about 45 minutes. Remove cover and bake another 5 minutes to brown the chickens.

Arrange on a preheated platter and garnish with parsley. Makes 4 servings.

chicken livers with apples and onion
hühnerleber mit äpfeln und zwiebeln

¾ pound chicken livers
3 tablespoons flour
½ teaspoon salt
¼ teaspoon pepper
⅛ teaspoon cayenne pepper
3 medium apples
¼ cup vegetable oil
¼ cup sugar
1 large onion, thinly sliced

Rinse chicken livers and drain on paper towels. Coat livers evenly with a mixture of flour, salt, pepper, and cayenne pepper. Set aside.

Wash and remove cores from apples. Cut apples into ½-inch slices, to form rings.

Heat 2 tablespoons vegetable oil in a frypan over medium heat. Add sliced apples and cook until lightly brown. Turn slices carefully and sprinkle with sugar. Cook uncovered over low heat until tender. Remove from pan and reserve.

Heat remaining 2 tablespoons vegetable oil over low heat. Add chicken livers and onion rings. Cook over medium heat, turning mixture often to brown all sides. Transfer to a warm serving platter.

Serve with apple rings. Makes 4 servings.

vegetables

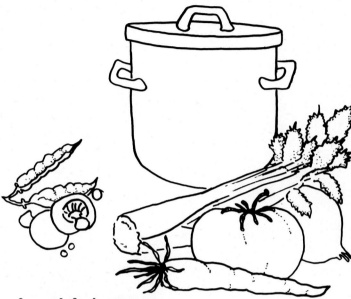

fresh asparagus
spargelgemüse

2 pounds fresh asparagus
(green or white)
Boiling salted water
¼ cup butter
3 tablespoons grated
Parmesan cheese
1 large hard-cooked egg

Wash asparagus spears and trim off tough ends. Place asparagus in boiling salted water and cook until tender, 7 to 9 minutes. Drain off liquid.

In a small saucepan, melt the butter; cook over low heat until lightly browned. Sprinkle cheese over butter; mix, and spoon over asparagus.

Garnish with sliced hard-cooked egg. Makes 6 servings.

white asparagus in white sauce
spargel in weisser sosse

2 14½-ounce cans white
asparagus
2 tablespoons margarine
2 tablespoons flour
½ cup reserved liquid
(from asparagus)

½ cup milk
4 ounces cooked lean ham, cut
into julienne strips
⅛ teaspoon nutmeg (freshly
ground if possible)
¼ teaspoon salt

Drain asparagus spears, reserving ½ cup of liquid.

Heat margarine in a saucepan. Add flour; blend. Gradually pour in asparagus liquid and milk. Stir constantly over low heat until sauce thickens and bubbles. Add ham and seasonings. Gently stir in asparagus spears; heat through, but do not boil.

Serve in a preheated serving dish. Make 4 servings.

green beans
with dill
grüne bohnen mit dill

1 9-ounce package frozen cut
   green beans
⅓ cup boiling water
1 beef bouillon cube
1 teaspoon dillweed or dillseed
2 tablespoons butter

Place frozen green beans in saucepan with boiling water, bouillon cube, and dill. Cover; bring to a boil. Separate beans with fork, reduce heat, and simmer 10 minutes or until tender. Drain. Stir in butter. Makes 3 to 4 servings.

brussels
sprouts
in beer
rosenkohl in bier gedünstet

1 pound fresh Brussels sprouts
Beer (enough to cover sprouts)
½ teaspoon salt
2 tablespoons butter

Trim and wash sprouts. Place in medium-size saucepan and pour over enough beer to cover. Bring to boil, reduce heat, and simmer for 20 minutes or until tender. Add more beer if needed, as liquid evaporates. Drain; add salt and butter. Serve hot. Makes 3 to 4 servings.

skillet
cabbage
gedünstetes weisskraut

2 tablespoons vegetable oil
3 cups finely shredded
   cabbage
1 cup chopped celery
1 small green pepper, chopped
1 small onion, chopped
½ teaspoon salt
¼ teaspoon pepper

Heat the oil in a large frypan about 20 minutes before serving time. Add ingredients and cook over medium to low heat about 15 minutes. Stir often. Cover pan during last 5 minutes of cooking time. Stir once or twice. Serve immediately. (Vegetables will be crisp.) Makes 4 servings.

sweet-and-
sour red cabbage
süss-saures rotkraut

¼ cup butter
4 medium apples, peeled and
   sliced
½ red onion, chopped
1 head red cabbage, finely
   shredded
1 cup red wine
4 whole cloves
⅓ cup brown sugar
2 bay leaves
¼ cup vinegar
¼ cup butter
Juice of ½ lemon

Melt butter in 4-quart Dutch oven. Add apples and onions; sauté slightly. Add cabbage, red wine, cloves, sugar, and bay leaves. Simmer, covered, for 1 hour, then add the remaining ingredients. Heat to melt the butter and serve immediately. Makes 6 servings.

red cabbage
rotkohl

2 tablespoons vegetable oil
2 small onions, sliced
2 pounds red cabbage,
   shredded
2 tablespoons vinegar
Salt to taste
1 teaspoon sugar
1 large tart apple, peeled,
   cored, and finely chopped,
   or ½ cup applesauce
½ cup red wine
½ cup hot beef broth

Heat oil in a Dutch oven and sauté onions 3 minutes. Add cabbage and immediately pour vinegar over cabbage to prevent it from losing its red color. Sprinkle with salt and sugar. Add chopped apple or applesauce and piece of salt pork. Pour in red wine and hot beef broth. Cover and simmer for 45 to 60 minutes. Cabbage should be just tender, not soft. Shortly before end of cooking time, remove salt pork; cube and return it to cabbage if desired. Correct seasonings and serve. Makes 4 servings.

red cabbage

westphalian cabbage

kohl westfälisch

1 head cabbage,
  approximately 2 pounds
3 tablespoons vegetable oil
1 teaspoon salt
1 teaspoon caraway seeds
1 cup hot beef broth
2 to 3 small tart apples
1 tablespoon cornstarch
2 tablespoons cold water
3 tablespoons red wine
  vinegar
¼ teaspoon sugar

Shred cabbage.

Heat vegetable oil in Dutch oven, add cabbage, and sauté for 5 minutes. Season with salt and caraway seeds. Pour in beef broth, cover, and simmer over low heat about 15 minutes.

Meanwhile, peel, quarter, core, and cut apples into thin wedges. Add to cabbage and simmer for another 30 minutes.

Blend cornstarch with cold water, add to cabbage, and stir until thickened and bubbly.

Season with vinegar and sugar just before serving. Makes 4 to 6 servings.

westphalian cabbage

carrots in beer
karotten in bier gedünstet

4 large carrots
1 tablespoon butter
1 cup dark beer
¼ teaspoon salt
1 teaspoon sugar

Peel and slice carrots into long, thin slices.

Melt butter in medium-size frypan; add beer and carrots. Cook slowly until tender, stirring frequently. Stir in salt and sugar. Cook for another 2 minutes and serve hot. Makes 4 servings.

mushrooms in cream sauce
pilze in sahnesosse

1½ to 2 pounds fresh
  mushrooms
¼ pound bacon, diced
¼ cup butter or margarine
2 large onions, diced
1 cup white wine
½ teaspoon salt

¼ teaspoon pepper
¼ teaspoon paprika
Pinch of nutmeg
Pinch of mace
1 cup heavy cream
Juice from ½ lemon
2 sprigs parsley

Clean mushrooms and slice in half if large. Pat dry.

Fry the bacon in a large pan until lightly browned. Remove from pan and reserve.

Add the butter to the pan drippings. Add onions; sauté until lightly browned. Add mushrooms; cook until tender, stirring often. Stir in wine, salt, pepper, paprika, nutmeg, and mace. Cover frypan and cook over low heat 15 minutes.

Off the heat, add the cooked bacon, cream, and lemon juice. Reheat until just warm. Do not let the mixture boil!

Garnish with parsley and serve with noodles or dumplings. Makes 4 to 6 servings.

marinated tomatoes
marinierte tomaten

4 large tomatoes, peeled and
  sliced
1 cup vegetable oil
¼ cup wine vinegar
¼ teaspoon dry mustard
1 teaspoon salt
¼ teaspoon black pepper

1 large clove garlic, minced
1 tablespoon chopped fresh
  basil
2 sprigs fresh thyme, chopped
1 sprig fresh marjoram,
  chopped
1 tablespoon minced scallion

Place tomato slices in serving bowl. Combine remaining ingredients and pour over tomatoes. Toss lightly. Chill for 1 hour or longer before serving. Makes 4 servings.

sweet-and-sour potatoes
süss-saures kartoffelgemüse

6 to 8 new potatoes, boiled in
  skins
1 medium onion, diced
¼ teaspoon salt

¼ teaspoon pepper
¾ cup sugar
4 slices bacon, cut up
¾ cup vinegar

Peel and cube potatoes. Add diced onion, salt, pepper, and sugar. Reserve in a covered bowl.

In a small frypan fry the bacon until crisp. Add the vinegar to the hot bacon and bring to a boil. Pour immediately over potato mixture; mix well. If too tart, add a little more sugar before serving.

Cut endive or leaf lettuce added to this is very good. Makes 4 to 6 servings.

yellow split-pea puree
erbsenpüree

1 pound (2 cups) dried yellow split peas
6 cups water or stock broth
1 large onion, whole
1 large carrot
1 large turnip or parsnip
⅛ teaspoon dried marjoram
⅛ teaspoon dried thyme
1 teaspoon salt
1 small onion, minced
2 tablespoons butter, melted
2 tablespoons flour

Presoak peas, if necessary, according to package directions. Drain well, if presoaked.

In a large pot, add water or stock, whole onion, carrot, turnip or parsnip, marjoram, thyme, and salt. Cook until peas and vegetables are tender, about 1½ to 2 hours. Drain well.

Mash peas and vegetables in blender or press through a sieve.

In a small frying pan, sauté the minced onion in butter until lightly browned; blend in flour and cook about 2 minutes. Add to blended peas and vegetables. Beat until fluffy. Makes 6 to 8 servings.

mashed potatoes with horseradish cream
kartoffelpüree meerrettich

4 to 6 potatoes
Boiling water
½ teaspoon salt
2 tablespoons butter
Freshly ground pepper
½ cup sour cream
1 tablespoon horseradish
2 teaspoons minced parsley

Peel and quarter potatoes. Cook in boiling salted water in medium-size saucepan until tender; drain. Mash, adding 1 tablespoon butter and the pepper. Add sour cream, horseradish, and minced parsley. Whip as for mashed potatoes.

Place in serving bowl; top with 1 tablespoon melted butter. Makes 3 to 4 servings.

potato pancakes
kartoffelpfannkuchen

2 large potatoes (grated on medium grater, makes about 2½ cups)
3 cups water
1 teaspoon lemon juice
1 boiled potato, mashed
1 egg, beaten
2 tablespoons milk
½ teaspoon salt
6 to 8 tablespoons vegetable oil

Grate raw potatoes into water to which lemon juice has been added. Place potatoes in a strainer or cheesecloth and drain off liquid well.

Beat raw and cooked potatoes with egg, milk, and salt to form a batter.

Using 3 tablespoons oil for each batch, drop batter for 3 or 4 pancakes at a time into hot oil in large frypan. When firm on bottom side, loosen edges and turn. Brown other side. Remove, drain on paper towels, and keep warm. Continue until all batter is used. Serve immediately.

If potato cakes are served with meat, sprinkle with salt. Sprinkle with sugar if served with applesauce. Makes 8 to 10 pancakes, or 3 to 4 servings.

salads

green-bean salad
schnittbohnensalat

1 pound fresh green beans, cut lengthwise
Boiling salted water
¼ cup stock reserved from green-bean cookery

3 tablespoons vinegar
3 tablespoons vegetable oil
2 medium onions, thinly sliced
½ teaspoon dried dillseed
1 teaspoon sugar

Cook beans in boiling salted water until just tender. Reserve ¼ cup of the cooking liquid and drain off the rest.

Prepare sauce by combining vinegar, oil, reserved vegetable stock, onions, dill, and sugar; stir until blended. Pour mixture over beans; marinate several hours before serving. Makes 4 to 6 servings.

red-beet salad
rote rübensalat

2 bunches red beets

marinade

2 tablespoons water
¼ cup vinegar
2 teaspoons caraway seeds
1 teaspoon sugar
2 tablespoons minced onion

1 teaspoon horseradish
¼ teaspoon ground cloves
½ teaspoon salt
¼ teaspoon pepper
5 tablespoons vegetable oil

Wash beets, trim off greens, place in medium saucepan, and cook, without peeling, in salted water to cover, until beets are tender. Peel and slice.

Prepare marinade dressing by combining remaining ingredients. Pour over beets and let stand for several hours before serving. Stir beets occasionally. Makes 6 servings.

cabbage fruit salad with sour-cream dressing
rohkostsalat

2 cups shredded raw cabbage
1 red apple, diced (do not peel)
1 tablespoon lemon juice
½ cup raisins
¼ cup pineapple juice
1½ teaspoon lemon juice
¼ teaspoon salt
1 tablespoon sugar
½ cup sour cream

Prepare cabbage and apple. Use 1 tablespoon lemon juice to wet diced apples to prevent darkening. Toss cabbage, apples, and raisins.

Mix fruit juices, salt, and sugar. Add sour cream; stir until smooth. Add to salad and chill. Makes 4 servings.

red-cabbage salad
rotkrautsalat

5 slices bacon
1 teaspoon sugar
2 tablespoons vinegar
¼ cup red or white wine
½ head red cabbage, shredded
2 tablespoons vegetable oil
½ teaspoon salt
¼ teaspoon pepper
1 teaspoon caraway seeds

Fry bacon in medium-size fry pan until crisp. Remove and reserve bacon.

Add sugar, vinegar, and wine to bacon fat; stir and cook until sugar is dissolved. Pour this hot mixture over the cabbage. Toss with vegetable oil, salt, pepper, and caraway seeds. Sprinkle crumbled bacon over mixture.

Serve at room temperature. Makes 4 to 6 servings.

cucumber relish salad
gurkensalat

2 medium cucumbers
1½ tablespoons sugar
1½ tablespoons cider vinegar
½ teaspoon salt
⅛ teaspoon pepper
½ cup sour cream
1 tablespoon minced fresh parsley

Slice cucumbers paper-thin. Sprinkle slices with sugar, vinegar, salt, and pepper. Marinate for 20 minutes, drain off liquid, and toss lightly with sour cream. Top with minced parsley. Makes 4 servings.

potato salad with beer dressing
kartoffelsalat mit biermarinade

6 medium potatoes
4 slices bacon
1 tablespoon chopped onion
1 stalk celery, chopped
1 teaspoon salt
2 tablespoons butter
2 tablespoons flour
½ teaspoon dry mustard
1 tablespoon sugar
1 cup beer
½ teaspoon Tabasco sauce
2 tablespoons chopped fresh parsley

Boil potatoes in medium-size saucepan until just tender. Peel and slice.

Fry bacon until crisp. Break into small pieces and mix with onion, celery, and salt; set aside.

Stir melted butter and flour in a small saucepan until blended. Add mustard and sugar. Slowly stir in beer and Tabasco sauce. Bring to boil, stirring constantly. Pour over potato mixture. Sprinkle with parsley. Toss lightly and let stand 1 hour.

Add bacon mixture; toss gently. Makes 4 servings.

bavarian
potato salad
bayrischer kartoffelsalat

This recipe is from a dear German landlady.

**4 cups potatoes, peeled and
   sliced ¼-inch thick
2 cups chicken broth, canned
   or homemade
½ teaspoons salt
¼ cup vegetable oil
⅓ cup chopped onion
½ teaspoon sugar
2 tablespoons lemon juice
Pepper, as desired**

Boil potatoes in broth with ¼ teasp-on salt for 5 to 8 minutes, until
tender. Drain. Toss warm potatoes with vegetable oil and onions.

Dissolve remaining ¼ teaspoon salt and the sugar in lemon juice. Pour
over potatoes. Marinate salad 1 to 2 hours before serving.

Serve at room temperature. Makes 4 to 6 servings.

cold
potato
salad
kalter kartoffelsalat

**6 large potatoes, peeled and
   quartered
Boiling water
½ teaspoon salt
1 medium onion, minced**

**3 tablespoons vinegar
½ teaspoon prepared mustard
1 teaspoon sugar
2 teaspoons dillseed**

In medium saucepan cook potatoes in boiling salted water until tender.
Drain, reserving ¾ cup of potato water. Dice potatoes. Add oil and
minced onion; toss gently.

In a small saucepan bring the ¾ cup potato water to a boil; pour over
potatoes and onion. Keep at room temperature for 2 to 3 hours.

Stir in vinegar, mustard, sugar, and dillseed. Potato salad will be creamy.

Serve at room temperature. Makes 6 servings.

hot
potato
salad
warmer kartoffelsalat

**3 medium potatoes, boiled in
   skins
3 slices bacon
¼ cup chopped onion
1 tablespoon flour
2 teaspoons sugar
¾ teaspoon salt
¼ teaspoon celery seeds
¼ teaspoon pepper
⅜ cup water
2½ tablespoons vinegar**

Peel potatoes and slice thin.

Sauté bacon slowly in a frypan, then drain on paper towels.

Sauté onion in bacon fat until golden brown. Blend in flour, sugar, salt,
celery seeds, and pepper. Cook over low heat, stirring until smooth and
bubbly. Remove from heat. Stir in water and vinegar. Heat to boiling,
stirring constantly. Boil for 1 minute. Carefully stir in the potatoes and
crumbled bacon bits. Remove from heat, cover, and let stand until ready
to serve. Makes 4 servings.

herring salad with sour cream
heringstopf mit saurer sahne

sour-cream sauce
1 cup sour cream
½ cup yogurt
Juice of ½ lemon
¼ teaspoon sugar

salad
2 small onions
2 tart apples
8 marinated herring fillets
2 teaspoons fresh dill or ½
   teaspoon dried dillweed

To prepare sauce, blend thoroughly sour cream, yogurt, lemon juice, and sugar.

Peel onions and cut into thin slices.

Peel and quarter apples, remove cores, and cut into thin wedges.

Blend onions and apples with sauce.

In a dish arrange herring and apple-onion mixture in layers. Cover tightly and marinate in refrigerator 5 hours.

Sprinkle with dill before serving. Makes 4 to 6 servings.

herring salad
heringsalat

1 8-ounce jar pickled herring,
   drained
½ green pepper, seeded and
   diced
1 tart apple, cored and diced
1 orange, sectioned and diced
2 teaspoons grated onion
2 tablespoons vegetable oil
1 tablespoon vinegar
Lettuce cups

Combine ingredients and marinate in refrigerator for at least 1 hour.
Serve on cupped lettuce leaves. Makes 4 servings.

fruit salad with nuts
fruchtsalat mit nüssen

1 small honeydew melon
2 oranges
1 cup blue grapes
Lettuce leaves
12 walnut halves

dressing
1 8-ounce container yogurt
1 tablespoon lemon juice
1 tablespoon orange juice
1 tablespoon tomato catsup
2 tablespoons evaporated milk
Dash of salt
Dash of white pepper

Scoop out melon with melon baller. Cut peel from oranges, remove white membrane, and slice crosswise. Cut grapes in half and remove seeds.
Line a glass bowl with lettuce leaves; arrange melon balls, orange slices, grapes, and walnuts in layers on top of lettuce.
Mix and blend well all ingredients for the dressing. Adjust seasonings.
Pour dressing over the fruit. Let salad ingredients marinate for 30 minutes.

Toss salad just before serving. Makes 4 to 6 servings.

herring salad with sour cream

fruit salad with nuts

hamburg-style fish salad
hamburger fischsalat

1 tablespoon butter
1 pound white fish fillets, fresh or frozen (cod, turbot, or haddock)
½ cup hot water
4 hard-cooked eggs
2 dill pickles
1 tablespoon capers

sauce
2 tablespoons mayonnaise
2 tablespoons sour cream
2 teaspoons lemon juice
1 teaspoon Dijon-style mustard
½ teaspoon salt
¼ teaspoon white pepper

garnish
1 hard-cooked egg
4 slices canned beets

Melt butter in a frypan. Place fish in frypan and pour hot water over fish. Bring to a boil, cover, lower heat, and simmer gently for 10 minutes.

Meanwhile, slice 4 hard-cooked eggs and the pickles.

Drain fish, cool, and cut into cubes.

Prepare salad sauce by blending mayonnaise, sour cream, lemon juice, mustard, salt, and pepper.

In a separate bowl gently mix fish cubes, egg and pickle slices, and capers. Arrange fish mixture in individual dishes and spoon salad sauce over tops. Chill for 30 minutes.

To garnish, cut remaining egg into eight pieces and chop beet slices. Arrange garnish on each serving. Serve immediately. Makes 4 servings.

hamburg-style fish salad

sauerkraut salad with ham

bavarian sausage salad
bayerischer wurstsalat

½ pound knockwurst, cooked
   and cooled
2 small pickles
1 onion
3 tablespoons vinegar
1 teaspoon strong mustard
   (Dijon or Gulden)
2 tablespoons vegetable oil
½ teaspoon salt
¼ teaspoon pepper
¼ teaspoon paprika
¼ teaspoon sugar
1 tablespoon capers
1 tablespoon chopped parsley

Cut the knockwurst into small cubes. Mince the pickles and onion.

Mix together the vinegar, mustard, and oil. Add salt, pepper, paprika, and sugar. Adjust seasonings if desired. Add the capers; mix well. Stir in the chopped knockwurst, pickles, and onions.

Just before serving, garnish with chopped parsley. Makes 4 servings.

tomato salad
tomatensalat

5 medium tomatoes, chopped
1 tablespoon sugar
1 teaspoon salt
1 teaspoon dried basil
¼ teaspoon dried thyme
¼ teaspoon freshly ground
   pepper
½ cup vegetable oil
6 tablespoons vinegar
1 tablespoon Worcestershire
   sauce
1 large onion, diced

Blend all ingredients together and chill for 1 hour before serving. Serve on lettuce. Makes 4 servings.

sauerkraut salad with ham
sauerkrautsalat mit schinken

1 16-ounce can sauerkraut
½ pound blue grapes
6 ounces cooked ham

dressing
½ cup yogurt
¼ teaspoon salt
¼ teaspoon white pepper
1 teaspoon honey

Rinse and drain sauerkraut; chop coarsely. Wash grapes and cut in half; remove seeds if desired. Cut ham in julienne strips. Gently mix these 3 ingredients.

Blend dressing ingredients and stir into sauerkraut mixture. Marinate for 10 minutes; adjust seasoning before serving, if necessary. Makes 4 servings.

breads, dumplings, and spaetzle

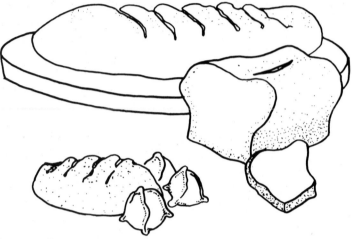

molasses brown bread
weizenkeimbrot

2½ cups whole-wheat flour
1½ cups wheat germ
⅓ cup brown sugar
½ teaspoon salt
1 cup raisins (mixed, light and dark)

2 teaspoons baking soda
1⅞ cup buttermilk
⅓ cup molasses

Preheat oven to 325°F. Grease a 9 x 5 x 3-inch pan.

Combine the flour, wheat germ, brown sugar, salt, and raisins in a mixing bowl. Mix well.

In a second mixing bowl mix baking soda, buttermilk, and molasses, using a wooden spoon. This mixture will start to bubble. Immediately stir it into the dry ingredients. Spoon the batter into the greased pan. Bake at once. The bread is done when a toothpick comes out clean, about 1 hour. Turn out of the pan and cool on a wire rack. Makes 1 loaf.

dill bread
dillbrot

1 package dry yeast
¼ cup warm water
1 cup creamed cottage cheese, heated to lukewarm
2 tablespoons sugar
1 tablespoon minced onion

1 tablespoon melted butter
1 egg
1 teaspoon salt
2 teaspoons dillseed
2¼ to 2½ cups flour

Dissolve yeast in warm water. Combine all ingredients in mixing bowl, except add flour a little at a time. Beat until well-mixed and mixture becomes a stiff dough. Cover and let rise in a warm place until doubled. Punch down and put dough in a bread pan, or arrange in a round shape on a greased cookie sheet. Let rise again. Bake for 30 to 45 minutes at 350°F.

While warm, brush loaf with soft butter; sprinkle well with salt. Makes 1 loaf.

rye
bread
roggenbrot

2 packages dry yeast
½ cup warm water
1½ cups lukewarm milk
2 tablespoons sugar
1 teaspoon salt
½ cup molasses
2 tablespoons butter
3¼ cups unsifted rye flour
2½ cups unsifted all-purpose
   white flour

Dissolve yeast in warm water.

In a large bowl combine milk, sugar, and salt. Use a mixer to beat in molasses, butter, yeast mixture, and 1 cup rye flour. Use a wooden spoon to mix in remaining rye flour. Add white flour by stirring until the dough is stiff enough to knead. Knead 5 to 10 minutes, adding flour as needed. If the dough sticks to your hands and the board, add more flour. Cover dough and let rise 1 to 1½ hours or until double.

Punch down dough and divide to form 2 round loaves. Let loaves rise on a greased baking sheet until double, about 1½ hours.

Preheat oven to 375°F. Bake 30 to 35 minutes. Makes 2 loaves.

old-country
rye bread
bavernbrot

A moist rye bread—full of flavor!

2 cups rye flour
¼ cup cocoa
2 yeast cakes
1½ cups warm water
½ cup light molasses
2 tablespoons caraway seeds
2 teaspoons salt
2½ tablespoons butter
2½ cups whole-wheat flour
   (more may be needed)
2 tablespoons cornmeal

Combine rye flour and cocoa. Do not sift.

Dissolve yeast in ½ cup warm water.

In a large bowl combine remaining water, molasses, caraway seeds, and salt. Stir well. Add the rye flour and cocoa mixture, dissolved yeast, butter, and 1 cup whole-wheat flour. Beat until dough is smooth. Spread remaining flour on breadboard. Turn out dough; knead flour into dough. If necessary, add more flour and knead until dough is elastic and smooth. Place in greased bowl, cover, and let rise until doubled.

Punch down dough, shape into a round or oval loaf, and place on greased cookie sheet that has been dusted with cornmeal. Let rise about 45 to 50 minutes.

Bake at 375°F for 35 to 40 minutes. Makes 1 large loaf.

spaetzle noodles
spätzle

3 cups flour
1 teaspoon salt
¼ teaspoon nutmeg
4 eggs, beaten
½ cup water (or more)
¼ cup butter

Sift flour, salt, and nutmeg together in a bowl. Pour eggs and ¼ cup water into middle of flour mixture; beat with a wooden spoon. Add enough water to make the dough slightly sticky, yet keeping it elastic and stiff.

Using a spaetzle machine or a colander with medium holes, press the noodles into a large pot full of boiling salted water. Cook noodles in the water about 5 minutes or until they rise to the surface. Lift noodles out and drain on paper towels.

Brown noodles in melted butter over low heat. Makes 4 to 5 servings.

spaetzle cheese noodles
käsespätzle

3 tablespoons butter or margarine
3 onions, sliced in small rings
3 ounces Emmenthaler cheese, grated

1 teaspoon dry mustard
2 cups cooked spaetzle noodles or thin noodles (see recipe for spaetzle)
2 tablespoons chopped chives

Heat butter in a frypan, add onions, and brown lightly.

Toss cheese with dry mustard. Add cooked noodles to cooked onions and cheese; mix well. Place mixture in an ovenproof casserole. Bake at 300°F for 20 to 30 minutes or until hot and bubbly.

Sprinkle top with chopped chives before serving. Makes 4 servings.

cooked potato dumplings
gekochte kartoffelklösse

6 medium potatoes, cooked in skins
½ to 1 cup flour
2 eggs, beaten
1 teaspoon salt
1 cup day-old white bread crumbs sautéed in ½ cup melted butter or margarine
6 to 8 cups hot beef or chicken broth
½ cup melted butter

Peel and grate potatoes while warm. Blend in flour, eggs, and salt to form a dough stiff enough to shape with fingers. Shape into balls 2 or 3 inches in diameter. If dumplings do not shape well, add more flour to dough. Force a few fried bread crumbs into the center of each ball; seal over. Reserve rest of crumbs.

Cook dumplings in boiling broth until they rise to the top, about 10 minutes.

Spoon melted butter over tops; sprinkle with remaining fried bread crumbs. Makes 4 to 6 servings—8 to 12 dumplings, depending on size.

cookies

brown-sugar cookies
braune zucker plätzchen

1½ cups brown sugar, firmly
  packed
⅔ cup shortening
2 eggs
2 tablespoons milk
1 tablespoon grated orange
  rind
2 teaspoons baking powder
1 teaspoon cinnamon
½ teaspoon cloves
¼ teaspoon salt
2 cups flour
1 cup raisins
½ cup chopped nuts, if
  desired

Cream sugar and shortening until light and fluffy. Beat in eggs, milk, and orange rind.

Sift together baking powder, spices, salt, and flour. Mix into sugar mixture. Stir in raisins and nuts.

Drop dough by teaspoonfuls onto greased cookie sheets. Bake at 350°F about 10 to 12 minutes, until done. Remove from baking sheets and cool cookies on rack. Store in airtight tins. Makes 4 to 5 dozen.

spice cookies
gewürzplätzchen

½ cup butter or margarine
¼ cup shortening
1 cup brown sugar, firmly packed
1 egg
¼ cup molasses
2½ cups unsifted flour
¼ teaspoon salt
2 teaspoons baking soda
1 teaspoon cinnamon
½ teaspoon ginger
½ teaspoon ground cloves
½ teaspoon ground allspice

Cream butter, shortening, and brown sugar thoroughly. Blend in egg and molasses.

Sift together remaining ingredients. Stir into sugar mixture. Shape dough into ¾-inch balls. Place 2 inches apart on greased baking sheet. Flatten each ball with bottom of glass that has been greased and dipped in sugar. Bake in preheated 350°F oven for 12 to 15 minutes. Cool cookies on racks.

Store in airtight tins. Makes 4 dozen.

spritz cookies
spritzgebäck

1 cup butter
⅔ cup confectioners' sugar
1 egg
1 egg yolk
1 teaspoon almond or lemon extract
2¼ cups unsifted flour
¼ teaspoon salt
½ teaspoon baking powder

Beat butter and sugar until light. Beat in egg, egg yolk, and extract.

Sift flour, salt, and baking powder. Gradually add flour mixture to eggs. Chill dough ½ hour.

Press ¼ of dough into cookie press. Keep remaining dough chilled. Shape cookies onto greased baking sheet. Bake in 400°F oven 7 to 10 minutes, until done. Cool on wire racks. Store in airtight tins. Makes 4 to 6 dozen.

almond crescents
mandel-halbmonde

1 cup butter or margarine
¾ cup sugar
1 teaspoon vanilla extract
1½ teaspoons almond extract
2½ cups flour
1 cup ground almonds
Confectioners' sugar

Beat together butter and sugar until very light and fluffy. Blend in extracts. Mix in flour and almonds.

Using about 1 tablespoon of dough for each, shape into logs and bend into crescents. Place on greased cookie sheet. Bake 12 to 15 minutes at 350°F, until light brown.

While warm, roll crescents in confectioners' sugar. Cool on racks. Store in a tightly sealed container. Makes 3 dozen.

nut
crescents
nusskipferl

1 package active dry yeast
4 cups unsifted flour
1 cup butter or margarine,
  softened
1 cup sour cream
3 egg yolks

filling
3 egg whites, beaten
1 cup ground nuts
1 cup sugar (or more, to taste)
1 teaspoon vanilla

Mix yeast, flour, butter, sour cream, and egg yolks thoroughly until dough is formed. Cover and let dough rest 1 hour.

For filling, beat egg whites until soft peaks form. Fold in nuts, sugar, and vanilla.

Roll dough ⅛ inch thick. Cut out rectangles about 2 x 3 inches. Spread with 1 teaspoon filling. Roll up jelly-roll fashion. Place on greased baking sheet and curve to form crescents. Bake at 350°F for 15 to 20 minutes, until lightly browned. Cool on wire racks. Store in airtight tins. Makes 4 to 5 dozen.

anise
drops
anisplätzchen

3 eggs
1 egg white
1 cup plus 2 tablespoons sugar
1¾ cups unsifted flour
½ teaspoon baking powder
⅛ teaspoon salt
1 to 1½ teaspoons anise
  extract

Beat eggs and egg white until very light and fluffy, about 5 minutes. Add sugar gradually; continue to beat for 20 minutes.

Sift flour, baking powder, and salt. Fold flour mixture and anise extract into beaten eggs. Make sure it is well-blended.

Drop by teaspoonfuls onto well-greased and floured baking sheet. Round cookies by using bowl of spoon. Let stand overnight. Cover with paper towel.

Bake at 325°F for 10 minutes, no longer. Cookies should not brown.

Store in covered tin. Cookies keep several weeks. Makes 4 to 5 dozen.

hazelnut
macaroons
haselnussmakronen

3 egg whites
¾ cup sugar
1 teaspoon almond extract
Pinch of salt

1 cup ground hazelnuts*
4 tablespoons cocoa
½ cup shredded coconut, if
  desired

Beat the egg whites until soft peaks form. Gradually beat in the sugar, 1 tablespoon at a time. Beat until stiff peaks form, about 5 minutes. Fold in almond extract and salt.

Mix the nuts, cocoa, and coconut. Fold into the egg whites.

Drop cookies by the tablespoon onto well-greased cookie sheets. Bake at 325°F for 15 minutes or until cookies are firm. Remove from baking sheet and cool on a wire rack. Store cookies in an airtight container. Makes 4 dozen.

*Hazelnuts (filberts) are available at gourmet or specialty stores. Remove skins by blanching for 10 minutes in boiling water and peeling. To grind, place about ¼ cup at a time in a blender, or chop very finely.

sand
tarts
sandtörtchen

2½ cups sugar
2 cups butter or margarine
2 eggs
4 cups unsifted flour
1 egg white, beaten
Sugar
Cinnamon
Pecan halves

Cream sugar and butter. Beat in 2 eggs. Gradually blend in flour. Chill dough overnight.

Roll as thin as possible on well-floured board. Work with ¼ of dough at a time. Keep remaining dough chilled. Cut into diamonds with a knife. Place on greased cookie sheets. Brush each cookie with beaten egg white. Sprinkle with sugar and a pinch of cinnamon. Place a pecan half in center of each cookie. Bake in preheated 350°F oven 8 to 10 minutes, until edges are lightly browned. Cool on cookie sheets 1 minute, then remove to wire racks.

Store in airtight tins. Makes 9 dozen.

spice
bars
lebkuchen

1 teaspoon cinnamon
1 teaspoon ground allspice
¼ teaspoon ground cloves
½ teaspoon salt
2¼ cups unsifted flour
½ teaspoon baking powder
½ cup ground almonds
1 teaspoon grated lemon rind
2 eggs
¾ cup sugar
¾ cup honey
½ cup milk

almond glaze
1 cup confectioners' sugar
½ teaspoon almond extract
1 teaspoon rum
1 to 2 tablespoons water

Sift together the spices, salt, flour, and baking powder. Stir in the almonds and lemon rind.

In a separate bowl beat the eggs and sugar until a ribbon is formed when the beater is removed. Stir in the honey and milk. Gardually stir in the flour mixture; beat until smooth.

Spread the batter in an 11 x 17-inch jelly-roll pan that is well-greased and floured. Bake at 400°F for 12 to 15 minutes, until the cake is done. While still warm, turn the cake out onto a rack.

To make the almond glaze, mix the confectioners' sugar, almond extract, rum, and 1 to 2 tablespoons water. Beat until glaze is smooth and of the right consistency. Add more water, if necessary, to thin.

Spread the warm cake with almond glaze. Cut cake into 1 x 2½-inch bars while still warm.

Spice bars keep 6 to 8 weeks in a sealed container if not glazed. Makes 4 dozen.

60

pepper balls
pfeffernüsse

4 cups unsifted flour
1 teaspoon baking powder
1 teaspoon cinnamon
1 teaspoon ground cloves
½ teaspoon mace
1 teaspoon ground allspice
Dash to ¼ teaspoon black
   pepper, if desired
1¼ cups honey
2 tablespoons butter
2 eggs
1 cup confectioners' sugar
1 teaspoon vanilla
1 to 2 tablespoons water

Sift flour, baking powder, and spices.

Heat honey and butter until butter melts. Cool to lukewarm and beat in eggs. Add flour mixture. Chill dough ½ hour.

Shape dough into 1-inch balls. Place on greased cookie sheet. Bake at 350°F for 15 minutes. Cool cookies on wire racks.

Mix confectioners sugar, vanilla, and water to form a thin glaze. Dip cookies in glaze and place on wire rack to dry. Store cookies in airtight tins. Makes 4 dozen.

desserts and cakes

apple pancakes
apfelpfannkuchen

⅔ cup unsifted flour
2 teaspoons sugar
¼ teaspoon salt
4 eggs, beaten
½ cup milk
2 cups apple slices
¾ cup butter or margarine
2 tablespoons sugar
¼ teaspoon cinnamon

Sift together flour, 2 teaspoons sugar, and salt.

Beat eggs and milk together. Gradually add flour mixture; beat until smooth.

Sauté apples in ¼ cup butter until tender.

Mix 2 tablespoons sugar and the cinnamon together; toss with apples.

Melt 2 tablespoons butter in 6-inch frypan. Pour in batter to a depth of about ¼ inch. When set, place ¼ of apples on top; cover with more batter. Fry pancake until lightly browned on both sides. Repeat procedure 3 times, until all batter and apples are used. Serve immediately. Makes 4 pancakes.

apple strudel
apfelstrudel

6 cups sliced tart apples
¾ cup raisins
1 tablespoon grated lemon rind
¾ cup sugar
2 teaspoons cinnamon

¾ cup ground almonds
½ box (16-ounce size) frozen fillo leaves, thawed*
1¾ cups butter or margarine, melted
1 cup fine bread crumbs

Mix apples with raisins, lemon rind, sugar, cinnamon, and almonds. Set aside.

Place 1 fillo leaf on a kitchen towel and brush with melted butter. Place a second leaf on top and brush with butter again. Repeat until 5 leaves have been used, using about ½ cup of butter.

Cook and stir the bread crumbs with ¼ cup butter until lightly browned. Sprinkle ⅜ cup crumbs on the layered fillo leaves.

Mound ½ of the filling in a 3-inch strip along the narrow edge of the fillo, leaving a 2-inch border. Lift towel, using it to roll leaves over apples, jelly-roll fashion. Brush strudel with butter after each turn. Using towel, place strudel on greased baking sheet. Brush top of the strudel with butter and sprinkle with 2 tablespoons crumbs. Repeat the entire procedure for the second strudel. Bake the strudels at 400°F for 20 to 25 minutes, until browned. Serve warm. Makes 2 strudels, 6 to 8 servings each.

*Frozen fillo leaves for strudel can be found at many supermarkets.

vanilla bavarian cream
bayerische vanillecreme

2 packages unflavored gelatin
½ cup cold water
9 tablespoons sugar
1 tablespoon cornstarch
2 eggs, beaten

1½ cup milk, scalded
1 cup vanilla ice cream
1 teaspoon vanilla
1 cup heavy cream, whipped

Sprinkle gelatin over cold water to soften. Heat to dissolve gelatin completely.

Mix together sugar and cornstarch. Add eggs; beat for 2 minutes. Slowly add warm milk, beating constantly. Pour into a 1-quart saucepan. Cook over medium heat until custard coats a spoon. Add gelatin and ice cream while custard is hot. Cool until slightly thickened. Add vanilla. Fold in whipped cream. Pour into 1-quart mold. Chill until set.

Unmold carefully and served garnished with fresh fruit. Makes 6 to 8 servings.

strawberry bavarian
bayerische erdbeercreme

1 quart fresh strawberries
¾ cup sugar
1 tablespoon gelatin (1 envelope)

½ cup cold water
2 teaspoons lemon juice
1 cup heavy cream, whipped

Slice strawberries and mix with sugar. Let stand until sugar dissolves.

Sprinkle gelatin over cold water. Let stand 5 minutes, then heat gently until gelatin dissolves completely. Add gelatin and lemon juice to sliced berries. Fold in whipped cream.

Pour into 1-quart mold or serving dish. Chill until set.

Unmold to serve. Makes 6 servings.

63

drop
donuts
tropfkrapfen

¼ cup soft butter
1 cup sugar
2 egg yolks, beaten
1 whole egg, beaten
4 cups flour

2 teaspoons baking powder
¼ teaspoon nutmeg
½ teaspoon soda
¾ cup buttermilk
Powdered sugar

Cream the butter and sugar. Stir in egg yolks and whole egg; blend.

In a separate bowl sift all dry ingredients except powdered sugar; add to creamed mixture, alternating with buttermilk. Stir to mix all ingredients.

Cook by dropping spoonfuls of dough into 375°F deep fat. Fry a few at a time, to keep fat temperature constant. Turn to brown on all sides. Drain on paper towels; sprinkle with powdered sugar. Makes 3 dozen.

jelly
doughnuts
berliner krapfen

3 to 4 cups unsifted flour
¼ cup sugar
1½ teaspoons salt
1¼ cups warm water (105 to 115°F)

1 package active dry yeast
2 egg yolks, beaten
¼ cup butter or margarine
Grated rind of 1 lemon
¼ cup plum or apricot jam

Mix 2 cups flour with sugar and salt. Make a well in the center and add ¼ cup warm water and the yeast. Allow to rise 20 minutes. Add egg yolks, remaining water, and butter. Beat until well-blended. Add lemon rind and remaining flour until a soft dough is formed.

Knead for 5 to 10 minutes, until dough is smooth and elastic. Place dough in a lightly greased bowl. Cover and let rise in a warm place until doubled in bulk, about 1½ hours.

Punch dough down. On lightly floured board roll dough ¼-inch thick. Cut dough into 2-inch rounds. On half of the rounds place about 1 teaspoon of jam or jelly. Moisten edges with water; place a second round on top. Press firmly to seal edges. Let rise 15 minutes.

Fry in deep fat heated to 375°F for 4 minutes on each side or until browned. Cut into first doughnut to be sure it's done in the center.

Drain on absorbent paper and sprinkle with lots of sugar, as the doughnuts are not sweet. Makes 24 doughnuts.

old german
muffins
altdeutsche brötchen

¾ cup butter or margarine
½ cup sugar
2 eggs
1 tablespoon rum
1 teaspoon vanilla
3 tablespoons milk
½ teaspoon cinnamon

2 teaspoons baking powder
2¼ cups flour
¼ cup ground almonds
1 tablespoon grated orange rind
¼ cup raisins, if desired

Cream butter and sugar. Beat in eggs, rum, vanilla, and milk.

Mix cinnamon, baking powder, and flour. Add flour mixture to butter mixture. Gently mix in almonds, orange rind, and raisins. Pour batter into greased muffin tins, filling half full. Bake at 375°F for 25 to 30 minutes, until browned. Makes 18 muffins.

red-wine jelly with fruit
rotweingelee mit früchten

Served as a dessert in Germany.

2 tablespoons (2 envelopes) unflavored gelatin
½ cup water
½ cup sugar
2 tablespoons lemon juice
3 cups dry red wine
2 cups fresh fruit, such as peaches, plums, strawberries, raspberries

Sprinkle the gelatin over the water. When gelatin is softened, heat gently to dissolve completely.

Add sugar and lemon juice to wine. Stir to dissolve sugar. While still warm, stir in the gelatin mixture. Chill until slightly thickened. Add fruit; mix gently to distribute fruit throughout. Pour into 1- to 1½-quart mold; chill until set.

Unmold to serve. Makes 10 to 12 servings.

cherry dessert meeresburg
meersburger kirschen-dessert

1 pound fresh tart cherries
3 tablespoons kirsch
6 tablespoons sugar
2 tablespoons water
12 ladyfingers
8 ounces cream cheese, softened to room temperature
½ teaspoon vanilla extract
2 ounces ground almonds (grind whole almonds in blender)
1 cup heavy cream
Chopped pistachio nuts for garnish

Wash and drain cherries. Remove stones but reserve 8 whole cherries for garnish. Place cherries in a bowl; add kirsch.

In a small pan boil 3 tablespoons sugar and the water for a minute to make a thin sugar syrup. Add syrup to cherries; stir to blend. Cover and let soak for 20 minutes.

Cut the ladyfingers in half, divide in 4 portions, and place in individual glass dishes. Arrange cherries on top.

Thoroughly blend cream cheese, 3 tablespoons sugar, vanilla extract, and ground almonds.

Whip the cream and carefully fold it into the cream-cheese mixture. Spoon over the cherries.

Garnish with the chopped pistachio nuts and whole cherries. Makes 4 servings.

swabian pancakes
fländle überbacken

This dish is generally a dessert, but, if preceded by a light soup, it may be served as a main dish for lunch.

1¼ cups flour
3 eggs
½ teaspoon salt
2 cups milk
1 teaspoon vegetable oil
1 16-ounce can applesauce
4 ounces raisins

1 teaspoon oil or butter (to grease dish)
2 tablespoons sugar
3 tablespoons sliced blanched almonds
1 tablespoon butter

Prepare pancake batter by blending flour, 2 eggs, ¼ teaspoon salt, and 1 cup milk. Lightly oil a large frypan and cook 6 to 8 pancakes (2 or 3 at a time).

Heat the applesauce and stir in the raisins. Divide the sauce between the pancakes and spread over each top. Roll up the pancakes like jelly rolls and cut each in half with a sharp knife.

Grease an ovenproof dish with oil or butter; place pancakes in the dish, setting them up on the cut edges.

Blend 1 egg with sugar, ¼ teaspoon salt, 1 cup milk, and sliced almonds. Pour over the pancakes. Dot with butter. Place in a preheated 375°F oven; bake for 40 minutes. Serve immediately. Makes 6 servings.

apple cake
blitzkuchen mit äpfeln

4 to 6 tart apples (medium size)
2 lemons, juiced
3 tablespoons sugar
3 tablespoons butter
¾ cup sugar
2 egg yolks (do not put 2 yolks together, as they will be used individually)
½ lemon, juiced and peel grated

1 teaspoon baking powder
1½ cups flour
¾ cup milk
1 tablespoon rum
2 egg whites
1 teaspoon butter (to grease cake pan)
1 teaspoon vegetable oil
3 tablespoons powdered sugar

Peel apples, cut in half, and core. Cut decorative lengthwise slits in apples, about ½ inch deep (see picture). Sprinkle with lemon juice and sugar. Set aside.

Cream butter and sugar together. One at a time, beat in egg yolks. Gradually beat in lemon juice and grated peel.

Sift baking powder and flour together. Gradually add to batter. Blend in milk and rum. In a small bowl beat egg whites until stiff. Fold into batter.

Generously grease a springform pan. Pour in batter and top with apple halves. Brush apples with oil. Bake in preheated 350°F oven 35 to 40 minutes.

Remove from pan and sprinkle with powdered sugar. Makes 6 servings.

Picture on opposite page: apple cake

black forest cherry cake

schwarzwälder kirschtorte

6 eggs
1 cup sugar
1 teaspoon vanilla
4 squares unsweetened baking
   chocolate, melted
1 cup sifted flour

syrup
¼ cup sugar
⅓ cup water
2 tablespoons kirsch

filling
1½ cups confectioners' sugar
⅓ cup unsalted butter
1 egg yolk
2 tablespoons kirsch liquer

topping
2 cups drained, canned sour
   cherries
2 tablespoons confectioners'
   sugar
1 cup heavy cream, whipped
8-ounce semisweet chocolate
   bar

Beat eggs, sugar, and vanilla together until thick and fluffy, about 10 minutes. Alternately fold chocolate and flour into the egg mixture, ending with flour.

Pour the batter into 3 8-inch round cake pans that have been well-greased and floured. Bake in a preheated 350°F oven 10 to 15 minutes, until a cake tester inserted in center comes out clean. Cool cakes in pans 5 minutes; turn out on racks to cool completely.

Make syrup by mixing together sugar and water and boiling for 5 minutes. When syrup has cooled, stir in kirsch.

Prick the cake layers and pour syrup over all 3 layers.

To make the butter-cream filling, beat together sugar and butter until well-blended. Add egg yolk; beat until light and fluffy, about 3 to 5 minutes. Fold in kirsch.

To assemble cake, place 1 layer on cake plate. Spread with the butter-cream filling.

Using ¾ cup cherries, which have been patted dry, drop cherries evenly over cream. Place second layer on cake. Repeat. Place third layer on top.

Fold 2 tablespoons confectioners' sugar into whipped cream. Cover sides and top of cake with whipped cream. Decorate top of cake with remaining ½ cup cherries.

To make chocolate curls from chocolate bar, shave bar (at room temperature) with vegetable peeler. Refrigerate curls until ready to use.

Press chocolate curls on sides of cake and sprinkle a few on top. Chill until serving time. Makes 8 to 10 servings.

frankfurt crown cake
frankfurter kranz

1 cup butter
1½ cups sugar
6 eggs, separated (egg yolks
    will be used one at a time,
    so keep them separated
    from each other)
1½ teaspoons grated lemon
    rind
8 tablespoons rum
4 teaspoons baking powder
3½ cups sifted flour

butter-cream filling
1 cup sugar
¾ cup water
6 egg yolks
1 tablespoon rum
1 cup unsalted butter

praline topping
2 tablespoons butter
1 cup sugar
½ cup water
1 cup blanched sliced almonds

apricot glaze
½ cup apricot jam

To prepare cake, cream butter and sugar until very light and fluffy, about 5 minutes. Beat in egg yolks, one at a time. Mix in lemon rind and 2 tablespoons rum.

Sift baking powder and flour together. Gently mix into butter mixture.

Beat egg whites until stiff but not dry. Gently fold the beaten egg whites into the batter. Pour into a well-greased 10-inch tube pan. Bake in a preheated 325°F oven about 60 minutes, until cake tests done. Cool cake in the pan 10 minutes, then turn out on wire rack to cool completely. Slice cake crosswise into 3 layers. Pour about 2 tablespoons rum over each layer.

For butter-cream filling, boil sugar and water to 238°F (soft-ball stage). Beat egg yolks until very light and fluffy, 5 to 10 minutes. While still beating the egg yolks, add the sugar syrup in a thin stream. Beat 5 minutes more, until very thick and doubled in bulk. Slowly beat in rum.

Beat the butter in a small bowl until soft and light. Beat butter into the egg mixture a little at a time. Continue beating until thick. Chill until mixture can be spread. If mixture is too soft, beat in additional butter.

While butter-cream is cooking, spread 2 tablespoons butter thickly in a 9 x 13-inch baking pan for praline topping. Then, in a 1-quart saucepan boil sugar and water to 238°F (soft ball stage). Stir in almonds; cook until mixture reaches 310°F or until syrup caramelizes. Pour syrup into prepared baking sheet. When cool, break up praline and grind it in a blender for a few seconds.

Finally, heat jam and press through a strainer or sieve to make apricot glaze.

To assemble cake, place bottom layer of cake on cake plate and spread with half of the butter cream. Repeat with second layer. Place third layer on top. Spread tops and sides of cake with apricot glaze. Press praline powder onto glaze. Any remaining butter cream can be used to decorate top of cake. Makes 10 to 12 servings.

crumb
cake
streuselkuchen

topping
¼ cup sugar
¼ cup brown sugar
2 teaspoons cinnamon
1 cup unsifted flour
½ cup butter or margarine

cake
2¼ to 2½ cups unsifted flour
¼ cup sugar
¼ teaspoon salt
1 package active dry yeast
¾ cup milk
½ cup butter or margarine
1 egg

For topping, mix sugars, cinnamon, and flour. Cut in butter until mixture is crumbly.

To make cake, mix 1 cup flour, sugar, salt, and yeast in a large bowl.

Place milk and butter in a saucepan and heat until very warm (120 to 130°F). Gradually add to dry ingredients; beat for 2 minutes. Beat in egg and 1 cup flour. Beat on high speed 2 minutes. Stir in remaining flour to make a stiff batter. Spread batter into well-greased 9-inch-square cake pan. Sprinkle with topping. Let rise in a warm place until double in bulk, about 1½ hours.

Bake at 350°F about 45 minutes or until done. Makes 1 9-inch cake.

golden
bundt
cake
rührkuchen

This rich moist cake needs no frosting and keeps well.

3 cups sugar
1 cup butter or margarine
½ cup shortening
5 eggs
3 cups unsifted flour
¼ teaspoon salt
5-ounce can evaporated milk
 plus water to make 1 cup
2 tablespoons vanilla butter
 and nut flavoring

Beat sugar, butter, and shortening until light and fluffy, about 5 minutes. Beat in eggs, one at a time, beating well after each addition.

Mix flour and salt. Alternately add flour and milk, ending with flour. Fold in flavoring.

Bake in greased tube pan at 325°F for 1 hour and 45 minutes, until done. Start in cold oven. Do not open door. Remove from pan and cool on wire rack. Makes 10 to 12 servings.

apple and rum custard cake

rahmapfelkuchen

crust
1½ cups unsifted flour
5 tablespoons sugar
1 tablespoon grated lemon
  rind
⅔ cup butter or margarine
1 egg yolk
1 tablespoon milk

filling
½ cup soft bread crumbs
2 tablespoons melted butter or
  margarine
4 cups tart sliced apples
1 tablespooon lemon juice
¼ cup sugar
¼ cup raisins, soaked ½ hour
  in ¼ cup rum
3 eggs, beaten
⅓ cup sugar
1¾ cups milk

To make crust, mix flour, sugar, and lemon rind. Cut in butter or margarine until mixture resembles coarse crumbs. Add egg yolk and 1 tablespoon milk; mix gently to form a dough. Pat into bottom of 10-inch springform pan that has sides only greased. Press dough up sides of pan 1 inch.

Toss together bread crumbs and melted butter. Spread evenly over pastry crust. Toss apple slices, lemon juice, and ¼ cup sugar. Spread apples over crumbs. Drain raisins, reserving rum, and sprinkle raisins over apples. Bake in preheated 350°F oven for 15 minutes.

Beat eggs and sugar until thick and lemon-colored. Stir in milk and reserved rum. Pour custard over apples and bake for 45 to 60 minutes at 350°F until custard is set.

Cool completely before serving. Do not remove springform pan until cool. Makes 8 servings.

gugelhupf

1 package active dry yeast
1 cup milk, scalded and cooled
1 cup sugar
1 cup butter or margarine
5 eggs
1 teaspoon vanilla

Rind of 1 lemon, grated
¾ cup raisins
⅓ cup ground almonds
  (2-ounce package)
½ teaspoon salt
4 cups unsifted flour

Sprinkle yeast in milk to dissolve.

In a large bowl beat sugar and butter until light and fluffy. Beat in eggs, one at a time. Stir in vanilla, lemon rind, raisins, and almonds.

Mix salt and flour. Add milk and flour mixture alternately, ending with flour.

Grease a gugelhopf mold*, bundt pan, or tube pan. Pour batter into pan. Cover and let rise until doubled in bulk, about 2 hours.

Bake in preheated 375°F oven for 40 minutes, until browned and done. Serve warm with butter. Makes 8 to 10 servings.

*This bread is traditionally baked in a gugelhopf pan or turban-head pan. If these are unavailable, a bundt pan or tube pan works just as well.

apple and cream kuchen
apfelquarkkuchen

1 package active dry yeast
½ teaspoon salt
4 tablespoons sugar
2 to 2½ cups unsifted flour
¼ cup butter or margarine
½ cup milk
1 egg

filling
3 cups sliced tart apples
1 tablespoon lemon juice
1 teaspoon cinnamon
¾ cup sugar
2 tablespoons flour
8 ounces cream cheese, softened
1 egg

Mix yeast, salt, 4 tablespoons sugar, and ¾ cup flour.

Add butter to milk. Heat until very warm, 120 to 130°F. Gradually add milk to flour mixture. Beat for 2 minutes. Add egg and ½ cup flour. Beat with electric beater on high speed for 2 minutes. Mix in enough flour to form a soft dough. Knead for 5 to 10 minutes, until dough is smooth and elastic. Place in greased bowl and let rise 1 hour, until doubled in bulk.

Pat dough into well-greased 10-inch springform pan, pressing 1½ inches up the sides of the pan.

Toss apples with lemon juice, cinnamon, ¼ cup sugar, and 2 tablespoons flour. Arrange in rows on top of dough.

Beat together cream cheese, ½ cup sugar, and egg. Spread over apples. Let rise in warm place 1 hour.

Bake at 350°F for 30 minutes. Best when served warm. Makes 1 9-inch cake.

hazelnut torte
haselnusstorte

5 eggs, separated
¾ cup sugar
6 tablespoons water
1¾ cups sifted cake flour
1 teaspoon baking powder
1½ cups ground hazelnuts (filberts)*
1 teaspoon vanilla
2 tablespoons confectioners' sugar
1 cup heavy cream, whipped
Fresh strawberries, if desired

Beat the egg yolks and sugar until very light, about 5 minutes. Slowly add the water.

Sift the flour and baking powder together. Mix with 1 cup of the nuts. Fold the flour mixture into the egg yolks.

Beat the egg whites until soft peaks form. Gently fold the beaten whites into the batter. Pour into a greased and floured 10-inch springform pan. Bake at 375°F for 30 minutes or until cake tests done. Cool the cake on a rack. When completely cooled, split the cake into 2 layers.

Fold the vanilla, confectioners' sugar, and remaining ½ cup nuts into the whipped cream. Spread whipped cream between the 2 cake layers and on top of the cake. Chill until serving time.

Garnish with fresh strawberries, if desired. Makes 8 servings.

*Hazelnuts are available at specialty or gourmet stores. They should be blanched. To blanch, boil the nuts 5 minutes and, when cool enough to handle, remove the skins. To grind, place about ¼ cup at a time in a blender, or chop finely.

fruit torte
obsttorte

pastry
2 cups flour
¼ cup sugar
1 cup unsalted butter
2 egg yolks

filling
3 to 4 cups fresh, canned, or
   frozen fruit
½ cup sugar if fresh fruit is
   used
¼ cup water, if needed
2 tablespoons cornstarch

almond coating
1 egg white
1 tablespoon sugar
½ cup sliced toasted almonds

topping
2 tablespoons sugar
1 teaspoon vanilla
1 cup heavy cream, whipped

Mix flour and sugar. Cut in butter until mixture resembles coarse crumbs. Add egg yolks; mix to form dough. Press dough into bottom and sides of a 10-inch springform pan. Dough should come 1½ inches up sides. Bake in preheated 375°F oven 20 to 25 minutes, until pastry is firm and light brown.

Drain canned or frozen fruit, reserving juice. Crush 1 cup fresh fruit to make juice. Add sugar to fresh fruit and let stand ½ hour. Drain juice. Add water to make 1 cup.

Mix cornstarch and fruit juice. Cook over medium heat until thickened. Place whole fruit in baked pastry shell. Pour thickened fruit juice over top. Chill thoroughly. Carefully remove torte from springform pan.

Beat egg white until foamy. Gradually beat in the sugar. Beat until stiff peaks are formed. Spread the meringue around the outside of the pastry shell. Press in the almonds so they completely cover the sides.

Gently fold sugar and vanilla into whipped cream. Spread over fruit. Garnish with sliced toasted almonds, if desired.

Recipe makes 8 to 10 servings.

grape torte
weintraubentorte

dough
2 cups unsifted flour
⅔ cup sugar
¼ cup butter or margarine
1 whole egg
1 egg yolk
Grated rind of 1 lemon
⅛ teaspoon salt

topping
1 pound grapes
3 egg whites
6 tablespoons sugar
Juice of ½ lemon
4 ounces ground almonds

Sift flour and sugar into a medium-size bowl. Cut in butter or margarine until mixture resembles coarse crumbs. Add egg, egg yolk, lemon rind, and salt; mix with a fork to form dough. Cover dough and let rest in refrigerator 20 minutes.

Roll out dough into a circle; place in an ungreased springform pan. Form a 1-inch-high rim. Bake in preheated 350°F oven for 10 minutes.

Meanwhile, clean and halve the grapes, and remove seeds if necessary.

Beat egg whites until stiff; blend in sugar, lemon juice, and ground almonds. Carefully fold in the grapes.

Remove cake from the oven. Fill baked cake shell with grape mixture, return to the oven, and bake for another 30 minutes at 350°F. Remove cake from pan and cool on wire rack. Makes 8 servings.

lemon
torte
fugger

zitronenkuchen der fugger

"Fuggers," a family of businessmen in the middle ages, lived in the town of Augsburg. They were so famous and rich that even the German emperor borrowed money from them. This is one of their family recipes.

dough
1½ cups flour
⅛ teaspoon salt
¼ cup butter or margarine
1 whole egg
1 egg yolk

filling
6 ounces ground almonds
⅔ cup sugar
Grated rind of 1 lemon
Juice of 2 large lemons

topping
2 tablespoons milk
2 ounces slivered almonds

Sift flour and salt into a medium-size bowl. Cut in butter or margarine until mixture resembles coarse crumbs. Add egg and egg yolk; mix with a fork to form dough. Cover and refrigerate for 15 minutes.

To prepare the filling, mix thoroughly almonds, sugar, lemon rind, and lemon juice.

Roll out half of dough into a circle and place in a 10-inch springform pan, forming a ¾-inch-high rim. Prick dough with a fork in several places. Spoon in filling. Roll out rest of dough, place on filling, and pinch edges together. Prick dough with fork in a decorative spiral pattern. Brush cake with milk and sprinkle with slivered almonds, pressing almonds lightly into the dough. Place cake into a preheated 350°F oven and bake for 40 minutes. Remove cake from pan and cool on a wire rack.

The lemon flavor will intensify if cake is held 2 days before serving. (Wrapped in aluminum foil, cake keeps up to a week.) Makes 8 servings.

special~occasion dishes

new year's pretzels
neujahrspretzel

A traditional good-luck bread of German families at New Year's.

2 cups milk
½ cup butter or margarine
2 packages active dry yeast
2 teaspoons salt
½ cup sugar
7 to 7½ cups flour

2 eggs
1 cup confectioners' sugar
1 to 2 tablespoons water
1 teaspoon vanilla
¼ cup almonds, chopped

Heat milk and butter until very warm (120 to 130°F).

Mix yeast, salt, sugar, and 1 cup flour. Slowly beat into warm milk. Beat for 2 minutes. Add eggs and 1 cup flour. Beat for an additional 2 minutes. Add enough flour to form a soft dough. Knead until smooth and elastic, about 5 minutes. Place dough in a greased bowl. Let rise in a warm place until doubled in bulk, about 1 hour.

Punch dough down and let rise again until doubled (1 hour more).

Divide dough in half. Shape pretzel as follows: Roll dough into a rope about 30 inches long and 1½ inch in diameter. Cross the ends, leaving a large loop in the center. Flip loop back onto crossed ends to form a pretzel. Repeat with remaining dough.

Place pretzels on greased baking sheets. Let rise 15 minutes more. Bake at 375°F for 25 to 30 minutes, until golden brown. Cool on wire racks.

Mix confectioners' sugar, water, and vanilla to form a thin icing. Spread icing on pretzels and sprinkle with chopped almonds. Makes 2 large pretzels.

pretzels
pretzel

1 cake compressed yeast	4 cups flour
1½ cups warm water	1 large egg, beaten
1 teaspoon salt	Coarse salt
1 tablespoon sugar	

Dissolve yeast in warm water. Add salt and sugar to yeast mixture. Blend in flour and knead dough until smooth, about 7 or 8 minutes. Cover and let the dough rise until double in bulk. Punch down. Cut dough into small pieces and roll into ropes. Twist the ropes into pretzel shapes and place on a greased cookie sheet. Using a pastry brush, brush pretzels with egg and sprinkle with coarse salt. Allow pretzels to rise until almost double in bulk.

Bake at 425°F for 10 to 15 minutes or until browned. Best if eaten immediately. If not, store in airtight container. Makes 12 6-inch pretzels.

chocolate pretzels
schokoladenpretzel

½ cup butter or margarine	*cocoa frosting*
¼ cup sugar	2 tablespoons cocoa
1 egg, beaten	1¼ cups confectioners' sugar
1 teaspoon vanilla	2 tablespoons butter or
¼ cup milk	margarine, melted
¼ cup cocoa	½ teaspoon vanilla
2 cups unsifted flour	

Cream ½ cup butter and the sugar until light and fluffy. Beat in the egg, vanilla, and milk.

Sift cocoa and flour. Mix into butter mixture until thoroughly blended. Chill dough until firm enough to handle (about 30 minutes).

Using 2 tablespoons dough, roll a rope about 12 inches long between your hands. Shape into a pretzel as follows: Make a loop about 1½ inches in diameter by crossing the ends, leaving 1-inch tails. Flip the loop down over the crossed ends. Press firmly into place. Place pretzels on greased baking sheets. Bake at 350°F for about 10 minutes.

Make frosting in a small bowl. Mix cocoa and confectioners' sugar. Gradually stir in butter and vanilla. If frosting is too thick, thin with milk.

When pretzels are cool, spread with Cocoa Frosting. Makes 2 dozen.

molded christmas cookies
springerle

These traditional Christmas cookies are formed with special rolling pins or molds.

4 eggs, beaten	1 teaspoon anise extract
2 cups sugar	4½ cups sifted cake flour

Beat eggs until very light and fluffy. Gradually add sugar; beat for 15 minutes. Do not underbeat. Fold in anise extract and flour.

Roll dough ⅜-inch thick. Thoroughly flour springerle mold or rolling pin. Press molds firmly to dough. Cut cookies apart and place on greased and floured cookie sheet. Let dry overnight at room temperature, covered with paper towels, or uncovered.

Preheat oven to 375°F. Place cookies in oven and immediately reduce temperature to 300°F. Bake for 15 minutes. Cookies should not brown.

Store cookies 2 to 3 weeks to mellow flavor. These cookies are very hard and may be used for dunking in coffee, tea or cocoa.

For Christmas, paint designs with egg yolk colored with food coloring. Makes 6 dozen.

dresden stollen

A traditional Christmas bread, often given as a gift. This bread is moist and heavy and full of fruits. It keeps well.

½ cup raisins
½ cup currants
1 cup mixed candied fruit
½ cup candied cherries, cut in half
½ cup rum
5 cups flour
1 package active dry yeast
½ teaspoon salt
1 cup sugar
1 cup milk
½ cup butter or margarine
2 eggs
1 teaspoon vanilla
½ cup chopped hazelnuts, if desired
½ cup chopped almonds
¼ cup butter or margarine, melted
1 cup confectioners' sugar

Place fruits in a small bowl. Pour on rum and let stand 1 hour. Drain fruits and reserve rum. Pat fruits dry and toss with 2 tablespoons of the flour.

Mix yeast, 1 cup flour, salt, and ¾ cup sugar.

Heat milk and margarine until milk is 120 to 130°F (very warm). Beat milk and reserved rum into flour mixture. Beat for 2 minutes. Add eggs, vanilla, and an additional 1 cup flour. Beat for 2 minutes more. Add enough flour to make a soft dough. Knead for 5 to 10 minutes, until dough is smooth and elastic. Place dough in a lightly greased bowl. Cover and let dough rise until double in bulk, about 2 hours.

Punch dough down. Gently knead in candied fruits and nuts. Shape stollen. Divide dough in half. Roll one half into a rectangle 8 x 12 inches, about ½-inch thick. Brush with melted butter and sprinkle with 2 tablespoons sugar. Fold ⅓ of the dough to the center. Repeat with other side, overlapping about 1 inch. Place on greased baking sheet. Mold the loaf by tapering the ends to form an oval. Repeat with other half of dough. Brush top of loaves with melted butter. Let rise until doubled in bulk, about 1 hour.

Bake in preheated 375°F oven about 25 minutes, until golden brown and crusty.

When cool, sprinkle with confectioners' sugar, or make a glaze with 2 tablespoons water and the sugar. Makes 2 loaves.

christmas bread

christstollen or weihnachtsstollen

A festive Christmas treat or gift!

2 cups milk, scalded and cooled
1 teaspoon sugar
2 teaspoons salt
11 cups white flour (may require more)
2 cakes yeast dissolved in ¼ cup warm water
1 pound butter
1½ cups sugar
6 large eggs
⅓ cup rum or brandy
1 pound golden raisins

1 pound assorted candied fruits and peels
1 pound chopped walnuts or slivered blanched almonds
½ teaspoon mace
½ teaspoon nutmeg
Grated rind of 1 lemon
¼ cup melted butter for tops of loaves
⅓ cup rum or brandy for tops of loaves
¼ cup powdered sugar for tops of loaves

In medium-size saucepan combine milk, 1 teaspoon sugar, salt, 1 cup flour, and dissolved yeast. Blend, cover, and let stand until bubbly in texture.

Cream 1 pound of butter and 1½ cups sugar until fluffy. Add eggs and liquor; blend well. Stir in 5 cups of flour. Add yeast mixture.

Blend 1 cup flour with fruits and nuts. Add remaining flour and rest of dough ingredients, using enough flour for a firm dough. Mix well.

Turn dough onto a floured breadboard and knead thoroughly. Place in a large greased bowl, cover, brush with melted butter, and let rise until double in size.

Punch dough down and turn onto floured board again. Separate dough into 3 or 4 sections and shape each part into a thick oval shape. Fold one long side of loaf about ¾ of the way over the other and gently press edges together for traditional stollen shape. Place on greased cookie sheets and let loaves rise until doubled.

Brush loaves with melted butter. Bake at 350°F about 1 hour to 1 hour and 20 minutes, depending on size of loaves. If loaves brown too fast, cover tops with aluminum foil. When loaves are done, brush with melted butter and spoon over a little more rum or brandy and let soak in. Sprinkle thickly with powdered sugar.

Allow bread to mellow for 2 or 3 days before cutting. Slice thinly and serve with whipped butter. Keep well-wrapped. Makes 3 to 4 loaves.

fruited wine drink

bowle

4 cups fresh fruit, such as nectarines, peaches, apricots, strawberries, plums
2 tablespoons sugar

1 cup brandy
2 bottles dry white wine, chilled
1 bottle champagne, chilled

Mix fruit and sugar, then pour brandy over the fruit. Let marinate 24 hours or more.

Place fruit and brandy in a large punch bowl. Add wine and champagne. Mix.

Remove fruit from punch and serve in a separate dish with toothpicks. Ladle out bowle into punch cups. Keep chilled. Makes about 14 6-ounce punch-cup servings.

index

A

Almond
  Coating 73
  Crescents 58
  Glaze 60
Anise Drops 59
Apple
  Cake 66
  and Cream Kuchen 72
  Pancakes 62
  and Rum Custard Cake 71
  Strudel 63
Apples and Onion, Chicken Livers
  with 40
Apricot Glaze 69
Asparagus
  Bavarian Veal with 32
  Fresh 41
  White, in White Sauce 41

B

Baked Pork Chops 30
Baked Spinach with Cheese 15
Bamberger Meat and Cabbage Cas-
  serole 18
Bavarian
  Cream, Vanilla 63
  Potato Salad 49
  Sausage Salad 53
  Strawberry 63
  Veal 32
  Veal with Asparagus 32
Bean Salad, Green- 47
Bean Soup
  with Frankfurters 8
  Two- 7
  White 8
Beans, Green, with Dill 42
Beef
  Goulash 18
  Roast with Mushroom Stuffing 23
  Rolls 20
  Stew 23
  Strips and Carrots 25
Beefsteaks, German 25
Beer
  Brussels Sprouts in 42
  Carrots in 45
  Dressing, Potato Salad with 48
Beet Salad, Red- 47
Black Forest Cherry Cake 68
Black Forest Stew 39
Blue Trout 38
Bratwurst, Grilled 16
Bread
  Christmas 78
  Dill 54
  Molasses Brown 54
  Rye 55
  Rye, Old-Country 55
Broth 26
Brown Bread, Molasses 54
Brown-Sugar Cookies 57
Brussels Sprouts in Beer 42
Bundt Cake, Golden 70
Butter-Cream Filling 69

C

Cabbage
  and Bamberger Meat Casserole 18
  Fruit Salad with Sour-Cream
    Dressing 48

Hunter's Stew with 28
Red 43
Rolls, Stuffed 15
Salad, Red- 48
Skillet 42
Soup 8
Stuffed 28
Sweet-and-Sour Red 42
Westphalian 44
Cake
  Apple 66
  Apple and Rum Custard 71
  Black Forest Cherry 68
  Bundt, Golden 70
  Crumb 70
  Frankfurt Crown 69
Capers, Veal Cutlets with 36
Carrots, Beef Strips and 25
Carrots in Beer 45
Casserole, Bamberger Meat and
  Cabbage 18
Casserole, Pork Chop and Rice 29
Cauliflower, Meat Loaf with 24
Cheese, Baked Spinach with 15
Cheese Noodles, Spaetzle 56
Cherry
  Cake, Black Forest 68
  Dessert, Meeresburg 65
  Sauce, Veal Cutlets with 37
Chicken, Grandma's 40
Chicken Livers with Apples
  and Onion 40
Chocolate Pretzels 76
Christmas Bread 78
Christmas Cookies, Molded 76
Coating, Almond 73
Cocoa Frosting 76
Cold Potato Salad 49
Cooked Potato Dumplings 56
Cookies
  Brown-Sugar 57
  Christmas, Molded 76
  Spice 58
  Spritz 58
Cream
  and Apple Kuchen 72
  Bavarian, Vanilla 63
  Filling, Butter- 69
  Horseradish, Mashed Potatoes
    with 46
  Sauce, Mushrooms in 45
Crown Cake, Frankfurt 69
Crumb Cake 70
Cucumber and Potato Soup 12
Cucumber Relish Salad 48
Curry and Lemon, Veal Steaks
  with 33
Custard Cake, Apple and Rum 71

D

Dill Bread 54
Dill, Green Beans with 42
Donuts, Drop 64
Dough 73, 74
Doughnuts, Jelly 64
Dresden Stollen 77
Dressing 50, 53
  Beer, Potato Salad with 48
  Sour-Cream, Cabbage Fruit
    Salad with 48
Drop Donuts 64
Dumplings, Cooked Potato 56

E

Eggs in Green Sauce 16

F

Farmer's Breakfast 14
Filling 59, 68, 71, 72, 73, 74
  Butter-Cream 69
Fish Salad, Hamburg-Style 52
Frankfurt Crown Cake 69
Frankfurters, Bean Soup with 8
Frankfurters, Lentil Soup with 10
Fresh Asparagus 41
Fresh Tomato Soup 11
Frosting, Cocoa 76
Fruit
  Red-Wine Jelly with 65
  Salad, Cabbage, with Sour-
    Cream Dressing 48
  Salad with Nuts 50
  Torte 73
Fruited Wine Drink 78
Fugger, Lemon Torte 74

G

German
  Beefsteaks 25
  Meat Loaf 24
  Muffins, Old 64
Gingersnap Gravy, Sauerbraten
  with 21
Glaze, Almond 60
Glaze, Apricot 69
Golden Bundt Cake 70
Goulash, Beef 18
Goulash Soup 9
Grandma's Chicken 40
Grape Torte 73
Gravy 23, 26
  Gingersnap, Sauerbraten
    with 21
Green
  Bean Salad 47
  Beans with Dill 42
  Sauce, Eggs in 16
Grilled Bratwurst 16
Gugelhupf 71

H-I

Ham, Sauerkraut Salad with 53
Hamburg-Style Fish Salad 52
Hazelnut Macaroons 59
Hazelnut Torte 72
Herb Stuffing 34
Herring Salad 50
  with Sour Cream 50
Horseradish Cream, Mashed
  Potatoes with 46
Hot Potato Salad 49
Hunter's Stew 16
  with Cabbage 28

J

Jelly Doughnuts 64
Jelly, Red-Wine, with Fruit 65

K

Kale and Potato Soup 9
Kuchen, Apple and Cream 72

L

Lemon and Curry, Veal Steaks
  with 33
Lemon Torte Fugger 74

Lentil Soup 9
  with Frankfurters 10
Livers, Chicken, with Apples
  and Onion 40

M

Macaroons, Hazelnut 59
Madeira Sauce, Roast Pork
  with 28
Marinade 39, 47
Marinated Rabbit 39
Marinated Tomatoes 45
Mashed Potatoes with Horseradish
  Cream 46
Meat, Bamberger, and Cabbage
  Casserole 18
Meatballs 26
  Königsberg-Style 26
  Sauerbraten 26
Meat Loaf with Cauliflower 24
Meat Loaf, German 24
Molasses Brown Bread 54
Molded Christmas Cookies 76
Muffins, Old German 64
Mushroom Stuffing 23
Mushrooms in Cream Sauce 45

N

New Year's Pretzels 75
Noodles, Spaetzle 56
  Cheese 56
Nut Crescents 59
Nuts, Fruit Salad with 50

O

Old-Country Rye Bread 55
Old German Muffins 64
Onion
  Chicken Livers with Apples
    and 40
  Pie 13
  Sauce, Pork Chops in 30
Oxtail Soup 10

P-Q

Pancakes
  Apple 62
  Potato 46
  Swabian 66
Pastry 73
Pea, Yellow Split-, Puree 46
Pepper Balls 61
Pie, Onion 13
Pork
  Chop and Rice Casserole 29
  Ribs and Sauerkraut 31
  Roast with Madeira Sauce 28
Pork Chops
  Baked 30
  Dusseldorf 31
  in Onion Sauce 30
  Stuffed 31
Potato Dumplings, Cooked 56
Potato Pancakes 46
Potato Salad
  Bavarian 49
  with Beer Dressing 48
  Cold 49
  Hot 49
Potato Soup 12
  Cucumber and 12
  Kale and 9
Potatoes with Horseradish Cream,
  Mashed 46
Potatoes, Sweet-and-Sour 45

Praline Topping 69
Pretzels 76
  Chocolate 76
  New Year's 75
Puree, Yellow Split-Pea 46

R

Rabbit, Marinated 39
Ragout a la Berghoff 17
Red-Beet Salad 47
Red Cabbage 43
  Salad 48
  Sweet-and-Sour 42
Red-Wine Jelly with Fruit 65
Relish Salad, Cucumber 48
Rice and Pork Chop Casserole 29
Roast Beef with Mushroom
  Stuffing 23
Roast Pork with Madeira Sauce 28
Rum Custard Cake, Apple and 71
Rye Bread 55
  Old-Country 55

S

Salad
  Cabbage Fruit, with Sour-
    Cream Dressing 48
  Cucumber Relish 48
  Fish, Hamburg-Style 52
  Fruit, with Nuts 50
  Green-Bean 47
  Herring 50
  Herring, with Sour-Cream 50
  Red-Beet 47
  Red-Cabbage 48
  Sauerkraut, with Ham 53
  Sausage, Bavarian 53
  Tomato 53
Salad, Potato
  Bavarian 49
  with Beer Dressing 48
  Cold 49
  Hot 49
Sand Tarts 60
Sauce 24, 39, 52
  Cherry, Veal Cutlets with 37
  Cream, Mushrooms in 45
  Green, Eggs in 16
  Madeira, Roast Pork with 28
  Onion, Pork Chops in 30
  Sour-Cream 50
  Tomato 29
  White, White Asparagus in 41
Sauerbraten 21
  with Gingersnap Gravy 21
  Meatballs 26
Sauerkraut
  Pork Ribs and 31
  Salad with Ham 53
  Spareribs and 32
Sausage Salad, Bavarian 53
Skillet Cabbage 42
Soup
  Cabbage 8
  Goulash 9
  Kale and Potato 9
  Lentil 9
  Lentil with Frankfurters 10
  Oxtail 10
  Potato 12
  Potato and Cucumber 12
  Tomato, Fresh 11
Soup, Bean
  with Frankfurters 8
  Two- 7
  White 8
Sour-Cream Dressing, Cabbage
  Fruit Salad with 48

Sour-Cream Sauce 50
Spaetzle Noodles 56
  Cheese 56
Spareribs and Sauerkraut 32
Spice Bars 60
Spice Cookies 58
Spinach with Cheese, Baked 15
Split-Pea, Yellow, Puree 46
Spritz Cookies 58
Steaks
  Esterhazy 25
  Veal, with Lemon and Curry 33
  Veal, with Yogurt 33
Stew
  Beef 23
  Black Forest 39
  Hunter's 16
  Hunter's, with Cabbage 28
Stollen, Dresden 77
Strawberry Bavarian 63
Strudel, Apple 63
Stuffed
  Cabbage 28
  Cabbage Rolls 15
  Pork Chops 31
  Veal Breast 34
Stuffing, Herb 34
Stuffing, Mushroom 23
Swabian Pancakes 66
Sweet-and-Sour Potatoes 45
Sweet-and-Sour Red Cabbage 42
Syrup 68

T-U

Tarts, Sand 60
Tomato
  Salad 53
  Sauce 29
  Soup, Fresh 11
Tomatoes, Marinated 45
Topping 68, 70, 73, 74
  Praline 69
Torte
  Fruit 73
  Grape 73
  Hazelnut 72
  Lemon, Fugger 74
Trout, Blue 38
Two-Bean Soup 7

V

Vanilla Bavarian Cream 63
Veal
  Bavarian 32
  Bavarian with Asparagus 32
  Breast with Herb Stuffing 34
  Breast, Stuffed 34
  Cutlets with Capers 36
  Cutlets with Cherry Sauce 37
  Rounds with Vegetables 33
  Steaks with Lemon and Curry 33
  Steaks with Yogurt 33
Vegetables, Veal Rounds with 33

W-X

Westphalian Cabbage 44
White
  Asparagus in White Sauce 41
  Bean Soup 8
  Sauce, White Asparagus in 41
Wine Drink, Fruited 78
Wine, Red, Jelly with Fruit 65

Y-Z

Yellow Split-Pea Puree 46
Yogurt, Veal Steaks with 33